GIFTS
AND
EXCHANGE
MANUAL

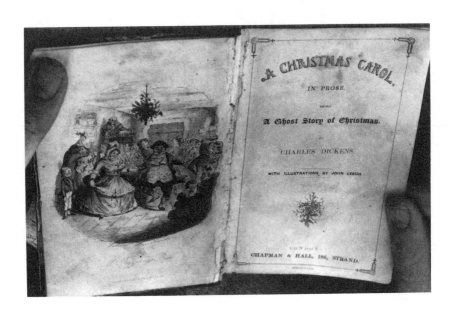

A rare first edition of Dickens' *A Christmas Carol.* Reprinted from the *Columbia Alumni News*, December 1951.

GIFTS AND EXCHANGE MANUAL

Alfred H. Lane

GREENWOOD PRESS **G P** | WESTPORT, CONNECTICUT

Library of Congress Cataloging in Publication Data

Lane, Alfred H
    Gifts and exchange manual.

    Includes index.
    1. Exchanges, Literary and scientific—Handbooks,
manuals, etc. 2. Libraries—Gifts, Legacies—Handbooks,
manuals, etc. I. Title.
Z690.L36   025.2'6   79-7590
ISBN 0-313-21389-5

Library of Congress Catalog Card Number: 79-7590
ISBN: 0-313-21389-5

First published in 1980

Greenwood Press
A division of Congressional Information Service, Inc.
51 Riverside Avenue, Westport, Connecticut 06880

Printed in the United States of America

10 9 8 7 6 5 4 3 2 1

Contents

Illustrations

Forms

Preface

It should be stated at the outset that this book is not intended to be a treatise or a scholarly examination of the philosophy of gift and exchange procedures. Nor does it attempt to examine the state of the art—although these points will not be overlooked entirely. Rather, this volume is intended to be a "how-to" book, a handbook of procedures. It will attempt to show what should be done to cope effectively with gifts to a library and to maintain an exchange program that will be useful and productive but will entail the least possible complications.

There is no one best way to operate a gift and exchange program. Circumstances will vary from library to library. In certain cases basic principles will be the same for all libraries; in other matters a choice of techniques is available. What is presented here is a series of suggestions that work. It is adaptation that is the key to making these suggestions useful in any given library situation.

Since the activities of gift work and exchange work are so similar, they are usually combined. In the following pages what is said about either area will probably apply to both, certainly in the organization and function of the unit if not in its actual mechanics.

Many people have aided and encouraged me in preparing this book, and I am grateful to them all. Special thanks go to Patricia Ballou and Jane Stevens for their many helpful suggestions; to Patricia Park for her dedicated work in the preparation of the manuscript; and to the Administration of the Columbia University Libraries in granting leave to work on this project. My thanks, too, to Lee Ash for permission to use samples of his gift appraisals.

GIFTS
AND
EXCHANGE
MANUAL

1

Organization

The function of a gift and exchange division (or department or section) of a library is to acquire library materials without direct purchase. As such, it naturally forms a part of the acquisitions unit. Terminology may differ, but the functions are the same. In this regard, the gift and exchange unit must maintain a high degree of cooperation with other departments of the library, notably the cataloging department (materials received and selected for inclusion must fit into the flow of cataloging activities), the reference department (some materials received will be reference items; reference books will be used for names, addresses, bibliographies, etc.), all readers' services (books and periodicals received must be serviced for reader use), and all book selection officers (their advice will be needed to determine what titles or types of materials should be requested or will be useful).

In actual practice, however, gift and exchange activities are not always carried on through the acquisitions department. Some libraries handle exchanges in the serials department, since so much of exchange material is serial in nature. In smaller libraries, exchanges are sometimes handled through the reference department or even through the librarian's office. Some librarians, too, feel that all gift activities should be handled through the librarian's office.

In any case, general exchange activity should be centered in one unit of the library. This is not to say that specific parts of an exchange program may not be carried on in other units. It may be useful or more efficient for language reasons (for example, in cases involving non-roman alphabets) or for reasons of geographic areas (Africa, Latin America, East Asia, etc.) to maintain exchanges through the offices of bibliographers or specialists. Government documents are frequently received either as gifts or exchanges, and these are most often handled separately from other gifts—usually through a documents unit. However, overall control should be centralized.

Suggested principles for the makeup of the unit indicate that there should be at least one professional librarian and as many subprofessional and clerical assistants as needed. The personnel should devote full time to the work of this unit. This, of course, may not be feasible in a small library where the degree of gift and exchange activity does not warrant full-time personnel.

Tauber has succinctly described the qualities needed in the personnel of a gift and exchange unit.

Whether or not the librarian is personally active in the gift operations, the personnel concerned with gifts have a strategic place in the acquisition program. The alert staff member in charge of gifts should know how to solicit gifts tactfully, how to acknowledge those items which are sent to the library by generous donors, how to publicize gifts, and how to coordinate the activities with acquisitions by purchase and exchange. Thus, the person involved should have qualities of initiative, energy, tact, ability to organize a program, and competence in the handling of clerical assistants.[1]

A word should be said as well about the value of foreign language ability in such a program. Although there do exist multilingual dictionaries of library terms, these should be relied upon only as backup reference tools. Although most European librarians are well enough versed in the English language to read exchange correspondence, they do not often write their letters in English. Thus, a basic background in one or more foreign language is very useful. It is also essential to be able to distinguish the words for editor, author, edition and even authors' names. There is the apocryphal story of the untutored librarian who listed a German book as being authored by "Auflage, Dritte." Obviously, such a situation is to be avoided.

The duties for which the staff of the gift and exchange unit are responsible include: (1) planning and organizing the work of the unit; (2) checking and claiming gifts and exchanges; (3) arranging and establishing new exchanges and canceling old ones when necessary; (4) centralizing all exchange activities and requests; (5) keeping all records and statistics; (6) deciding between gift or exchange and purchase; (7) organizing exchange of duplicates; (8) continually studying the exchange program; (9) accepting and recording gifts; (10) acknowledging gifts; (11) soliciting gifts; (12) publicizing gifts; and (13) arranging for dispersal of wanted items and disposing of unwanted items.

It should be noted that the handling of gifts and exchanges is not exclusively an intellectual process. The books received as gifts and exchange and the materials sent on exchange are actually *handled*— and not always one at a time. Gifts arrive in packages, boxes, crates, shopping bags and even trunks and barrels. Exchanges, too, can come and go in small and large quantities. Thus, the gift and exchange librarian should be aware that there is a physical side to be considered, and there may not always be an assistant available at the right time and place when a shipment is delivered or a full book truck must be moved.

Finally, an important factor to keep in mind is the public relations role of the gifts and exchange librarian. Since this librarian will be dealing with donors and potential donors as the representative of the library (and, indeed, of the parent institution) this responsibility should be reflected in the individual's dress, attitude, courtesy and tact, and judgment. A broad knowledge of his library's collecting policies is essential.

NOTE

1. Maurice F. Tauber and Associates, *Technical Services in Libraries,* Columbia University Studies in Library Service, no. 7 (New York: Columbia University Press, 1953), p. 83.

ADDITIONAL REFERENCES

Association of Research Libraries. Office of University Library Management Studies. Systems and Procedures Exchange Center (SPEC). "Gifts and Exchange Functions." SPEC Flyer and Kit, no. 28.
Kovacic, Mark. "The Organization and Function of Gift and Exchange Programs in Eighteen Selected U.S. Academic Libraries." 1977-78 Fellowship Study. Council on Library Resources, Washington, D.C.

2 | Introduction to Interlibrary Exchanges

The history of barter or exchange parallels the history of civilization. From mankind's earliest days, one who had something he did not want or need offered it to another for something he did need or want. At first this activity involved only the necessities of life: food, clothing, shelter, or the tools for providing these; but as time went on and civilization progressed, the range of exchangeable materials expanded. The interchange of knowledge became not only desirable but important and necessary. In the development of recorded knowledge, from the earliest chipped stones through the invention of the printing press to our present-day books and audio-visual materials, there is reflected the idea of exchange of knowledge. Today the exchange of library materials is of major importance to most large research libraries and, indeed, to many small libraries, too.

Interlibrary exchange started in Europe as early as the seventeenth century and in this country in the early nineteenth century. The French ventriloquist Alexander Vattemare, on his tours to various countries, often visited libraries and museums. He noted that these institutions often had duplicate books, documents, and art objects, and he had the idea that it would be beneficial if these items were exchanged between various countries. While in this country during 1839-41, he persuaded Congress to exchange some of our official publications with France. Although Vattemare's program in this country lasted only a few years, his basic ideas were sound and became the fundamentals for exchange programs as we know them today. International conferences on exchanges were held in the late 1800s and in the early years of the twentieth century and were mainly concerned with official government publications. Later conventions expanded their scope to include the exchange of art objects, bibliographies, and scientific and literary publications. Examples are the Convention Concerning the Exchange of Official, Scientific, Literary and Industrial Publications, signed January 27, 1902, in Mexico, and the Convention on Patents of Invention, Drawings and Industrial Models, Trade-Marks and Literary and Artistic Property (Copyright Laws and Treaties of the World— Multilateral Conventions—Rio de Janeiro Copyright Convention, 1906: Item 1), signed August 23, 1906, in Rio de Janeiro.[1] Perhaps the greatest influence on the growth of exchanges has been the United Nations Educational, Scientific and Cultural Organization (UNESCO).

Of no less importance was the influence of the International Exchange Service of the Smithsonian Institution. In 1848 the Smithsonian issued its first publication and distributed it to institutions in other countries. In 1867 the Smithsonian was authorized by Congress to ship U.S. documents to foreign countries. Since then it has acted as the transmittal agent for libraries, scientific societies, educational institutions and individuals wishing to distribute their publications abroad. Materials are packaged and addressed by the originating institution and are sent prepaid to the Smithsonian Institution. Here the packages are sorted by country and combined with similar shipments from other organizations. They are then forwarded to exchange centers in other countries which arrange to have the packages delivered to the addressees. Materials coming to the Smithsonian from other countries are similarly delivered free of charge to the addressees in this country.

NOTE

1. *Reunion de expertos sobre conje internacional de publicaciones en America Latina: Informe final,* comp. Marietta Daniels (Havana: UNESCO, 1956). The UNESCO *Handbook of International Exchanges* lists all multilateral agreements that have been opened for signature or have come into force in the fields of education, science, culture, and mass communications.

ADDITIONAL REFERENCES

Williams, E. E. and Noble, Ruth V. "Preliminary memoranda" in *Conference on International Cultural, Educational, and Scientific Exchanges at Princeton University, November 25-26, 1946.* Chicago: American Library Association, 1947. Pages 83-99 contain an excellent resume of early exchanges.

Virks, Gerda. "Bibliography on the History and Development of the Exchange of Publications, 1876-1957." M. L. S. thesis, Catholic University, 1959.

3 | Exchange Work in an Academic Library

WHY EXCHANGE?

The question is often asked, Why go through the bother of setting up an exchange program when you can buy the same materials through established purchase channels? The answer is complex, and it is difficult to establish which elements are more important than others. Let us start with the fact that many items, both monographs and serial titles, are not available in any other way. This is especially true in some European countries. And these kinds of materials are the stuff of research. Examples might include dissertations, art exhibit catalogs, certain *Festschriften,* lecture notes, reports of special studies and investigations, monthly or quarterly reports of research projects, and the like. For example, in honor of the two hundredth anniversary of the founding of Columbia University the following *Festschrift* was published and was available only through gift or exchange: *Veritas Iustitia Libertas,* Festschrift zue 200-Jahrfeier der Columbia University New York, Ueberricht von der Freien Universitat Berlin und der Deutschen Hochschule fur Politik Berlin.

Another reason for exchange is the financial saving. Materials bought for exchange purposes are usually obtained at a library (or even a special) discount, whereas the value charged against the exchange partner is the retail price. This is not cheating; the partner is doing the same thing. Frequently a university press will give a portion of its output (or at least a special large discount) to the library for its exchange program. Periodical publications issued by the institution may be nominally free—or at least not charged to the library budget. For more on this see the section on available materials.

A special kind of reason for an exchange program is based on politics and economics. Certain countries (notably those in East Central Europe) put great restrictions on the export of dollars; thus, libraries in those countries *must* get their U.S. publications through exchange or gift. This necessity can work to great advantage for U.S. libraries. Publications of these countries have a lower dollar value than similar U.S. publications. Thus, what we send on exchange will bring more value in titles for dollars spent.

Keller in his "Memoranda on Library Cooperation" points out that "all libraries have some books which, to them, are a complete liability. They require housing, cataloging, and administration, and never pay dividends in terms of usage. These same books, if placed in other libraries, may be in active circulation, even filling in gaps difficult to bridge otherwise."[1] In other words, exchange is a useful way to dispose of duplicates, as well as other unwanted materials, such as books in subject areas not collected by the library.

WHAT IS AVAILABLE ON EXCHANGE?

Under certain conditions almost any kind of library material is available on exchange. The most frequently available are the publications of other academic institutions, learned societies, libraries, and governments. There are also the publications (monographic and serial) that are duplicates with the exchange partner. Sometimes it is possible to obtain commercially published titles that the partner is willing to buy.

Conversely, the same kinds of materials are available to send on exchange. In 1947 there were identified twelve categories of materials used by college and university libraries: (1) university catalogs, bulletins, and other official publications; (2) dissertations, whole or in abstract; (3) duplicate books; (4) duplicate serials; (5) non-duplicate materials; (6) university published serials, monographic; (7) university published journals; (8) university press publications; (9) department publications; (10) library publications; (11) society and institute publications; (12) miscellaneous materials, including such items as microfilm, catalogs, newspapers, and pamphlets.[2] These categories are still valid, with the possible exception of dissertations, which are now, for the most part, produced in microform.

Publications of university presses, while extremely valuable as exchange stock, may not now be so readily available without charge since production costs have risen so markedly in recent years. However, a substantial discount for exchange purposes should still be sought. It is wise to point out to the publishing agency that the use of these publications for exchange is not cutting into the press's market, for there is no market abroad if those countries cannot export currency.

There are several sources for learning of specific titles available on exchange. Primary among these is the *UNESCO Handbook on the International Exchange of Publications.* This book is especially useful for setting up new exchanges. It lists libraries and other institutions by country and tells what titles are available, where to write, and what kinds of materials they are interested in receiving.

Supplementing this handbook is the *UNESCO Bulletin for Libraries,* a journal which appears six times a year. In addition to articles and news notes on the world of exchange, each issue has a section on exchange, publications wanted, and items for free distribution.

Another useful tool is *The World of Learning,* which is a geographical listing of universities, learned societies, and other organizations, with names of individual officers and faculty and frequently indicates publications issued.

In addition, often new titles which could be available on exchange appear in the literature of the library world as well as in various subject journals. Some examples of such journals are: *Journal of American History, TLA* (Theatre Library Association) *Broadside, Educational Theater Journal,* (New York State Library) *Bookmark, New Serial Titles,* and *Library Journal.* (See also Chapter 4 in this volume, "Gifts to Libraries").

SETTING UP AN EXCHANGE AGREEMENT

Agreement to exchange publications can be set up through a formal contract, a simple form letter, or an informal typed letter. No matter what format is used, there are certain basic facts to be stated explicitly. The exact mailing address for each partner must be indicated. The specific titles or general types of materials to be exchanged must be known. How materials are to be sent may be mentioned: by air mail for important dated matter, by regular sea mail to foreign countries, by special library rate in this country, or through a central exchange agency, such as the International Exchange Service of the Smithsonian Institution. Each partner will want to know the basis for exchange. Will it be piece-for-piece (for monographs), title-for-title (for serials), priced (value-for-value), or lot-for-lot (everything available for everything available)? Some libraries have asked for exchanges based on the number of pages sent and received. Silly as this idea seems, it does have validity. Obviously, the exchange of twenty-five items for twenty-five items is not balanced if one partner sends only pamphlets while the other sends large volumes.

The usual pattern in setting up an exchange arrangement is to write a letter to the proposed exchange partner outlining one's fields of interest and the materials available for exchange and proposing a basis for the exchange. One can ask at this time to receive a specific title or group of materials (for example, catalogs of exhibitions or publications in the field of anthropology) in exchange for similar titles. When offering a serial title, it is helpful to send a sample issue for examination by the proposed partner. This informal arrangement by letter is most often successful if the pattern of operation is stated properly and fully. The choice of exchange partners should involve consideration of the library's collecting policies, subject fields, and languages.

In some cases, a formal contract is offered in which terms are specifically stated (including provision for breaking off the exchange if later desired) and signed by both parties. Such a formal arrangement is seldom necessary. The following is a sample of such a contract in which, unfortunately, the terms of termination were not spelled out.

EXCHANGE AGREEMENT BETWEEN COLUMBIA UNIVERSITY LIBRARIES AND LAS BIBLIOTECAS DEL CONSEJO SUPERIOR DE INVESTIGACIONES CIENTIFICAS

This agreement is a statement of the basic principles upon which the exchange relations between the Libraries of Columbia University and El Consejo Superior de Investigaciones Cientificas is to be founded.

1. This agreement is to apply only between the two above-mentioned institutions and is not meant to preclude relations with other libraries or institutions.
2. Exchange will be effected on a "priced" or value basis; that is, each institution will send materials to the other, indicating the market value of those materials in American dollars. Records will be kept of items received and sent. Adjustments of the balance will be made by the further exchange of publications (printed, or reproduced by a photographic process).
3. All transportation of exchange materials will be handled through the Smithsonian Institution and International Exchange Bureau in the respective countries. Each contracting institution will pay

the costs of transportation within its own country.

4. Materials to be exchanged will include from the Consejo, publications of the Consejo and other materials of Spanish origin, including the publications of agencies of the Spanish government, as they may be available; from Columbia, materials for exchange will be limited to items on specific lists which will be sent from time to time for this purpose. These lists will include United States government publications. Columbia University will not undertake to supply materials from commercial publishers in this country on exchange, except as they may become available for that purpose.

5. Materials received by the Consejo on exchange from Columbia and which duplicate holdings in the Consejo or which do not readily fit into the collections of the Consejo will be distributed to other interested libraries in Spain and will be credited to Columbia's exchange account.

6. This contract is being written in English and Spanish. In case of controversy the English version will be taken as the true version.

7. Materials sent on exchange to the Consejo will be addressed as follows:

    Materials sent on exchange to Columbia will be addressed as follows:

If the exchange is to be on a priced basis, it would be wise to agree on the monetary exchange rate to be used. By definition it is implied that the exchange will attain an overall balance. It would be illogical to send a title that has a current subscription price of ten dollars per year and receive in return a journal that sells for ten Swiss francs (about one-half the value of the U.S. subscription). It is doubtful that the day-by-day fluctuations in the money market will have any real effect on the exchange values, but it is wise to review exchange rates about once a year, or more often if world events so indicate.

On the other hand, if it is agreed that exchange will be on a piece-for-piece basis, it is not necessary that each partner send exactly twenty-five pieces each year, for instance. It could be that one partner sent twelve pieces and received forty-eight pieces one year, but the balance might be reversed the following year. It is the relatively long-range picture that counts.

EXCHANGE RECORDS

Certain records are vital to an efficient exchange operation. They should be accurate and simple but adequate. Basic information records would include statistics (only if they serve a useful purpose), number and value of materials sent and received, monies spent for materials purchased for exchange, and perhaps subject profiles of exchange partners' interests. More specifically, for serials received one should know:

1. The title in its original language
2. The English translation of the title
3. Date of request on exchange or date of cancellation
4. Frequency of publication
5. Destination within the receiving library
6. Subscription cost and cost of individual issues

In many libraries, records and paper work are duplicated in various ways from department to department when one such record would be sufficient. The physical formats for these records may vary from loose-leaf notebooks to file folders to various types and sizes of card files. For other than correspondence, the most common format is the 3-x-5-inch or 5-x-8-inch card file listing the mailing address (sometimes an address for shipments and another for correspondence), interest profile, titles of serials sent and received, and dates and numbers of monographs sent and received. A *brief* history of the exchange could be included showing the date of origination and references to important correspondence. Most of these records should be kept indefinitely, although routine form requests, claims, acknowledgments, and so forth could be weeded after a short time, and correspondence older than five years could be retired to a storage area.

The filing scheme for these various records differs from library to library. In some libraries, filing is by the official cataloging entry of the institution. In other libraries, exchange partners are broken down first by country, then by name of the institution. Some libraries assign alpha-numeric codes to exchange partners, and all filing arrangements are by this code. At least one library arranges domestic libraries by the name of the institution and foreign libraries by the name of the city where each is located. Which system is adopted is less important than ensuring that those concerned know the system and that the system is consistent.

It would seem self-evident that some kind of record should be kept of all items requested together with the date of the request. There are several reasons for this record: to identify the material when it arrives, to initiate a follow-up if necessary, and to note whether all items requested have been received and whether the received material is indeed what was requested.

PAPER WORK

One of the characteristics of exchange work is the high volume of correspondence. Form letters can do much to alleviate this burden and also help keep costs down. It was not so many years ago that the form letter was frowned upon as being too impersonal, but in today's mechanized world even a computer-generated letter is considered quite acceptable and businesslike. Wherever information to be conveyed is repetitive, a form (or computer-issued) letter is in order. Such letters might include a request for items from an exchange offer list; a multiple-answer letter to be checked with the appropriate response to a query or a problem; a request to stop sending a serial title or to change the address being used. Samples of such form letters appear in Appendix E.

Acknowledgments are another form of paper work to be considered. Materials for which a specific request has been made should be acknowledged; usually a post card will suffice. In terms of periodicals received regularly, acknowledgment is not usually necessary unless a form for this purpose is enclosed with the shipment. Duplicated lists of exchange offers do not need to be acknowledged unless items are to be requested; in this case the list should be identified in the request by date, number, or descriptive title. A duplicated list, of course, is quite different from a specially prepared exchange list in conjunction with specific correspondence. Such a list does require an acknowledgment.

Other forms which would not be considered letters but which still convey a message would include claims for missing items, tracers on previous correspondence, acknowledgments for materials received, and announcements of unavailability of items requested. One caution: Be sure that the full and exact address of the sender appears conspicuously on the form and that there is a space to indicate any reference mark the respondent may wish to have cited.

Depending on the filing system used, most correspondence will employ a reference citation. This is especially true on letters from European countries. The reference may be a combination of letters and numerals, which may include the writer's initials, a symbol for the department or office of the institution, a date, a transaction number, or a symbol representing the library in their records. Thus, a reference expressed as Ex/US-CU/78/15/AHL might be translated to mean: Exchange/United States-Columbia University/1978/15th letter to this institution/initials of the writer. In any case, such references should be quoted in order that correspondence can be matched and also to ensure that mistakes will not be made.

A word should be said here about the value of dealing with an individual person in exchange correspondence. Over a period of time interpersonal contact can enhance the value of an exchange arrangement. On the other hand, personnel may change so rapidly that individual names may lose their effectiveness. A compromise would be to address the outer envelope to the office or title involved with the inner letter addressed to the attention of a particular individual.

Lists of materials offered on exchange should always include the exact address to which replies should be sent; an identifying word, code, number, or date to individualize the list; and instructions on how to request items, including time limit (if any), return of postage paid, and order in which requests will be filled. Mail to foreign countries usually takes much longer than domestic mail. Monographs should be listed separately from serials. Alphabetizing the list helps both sender and receiver even though the materials may be arranged numerically. For monographs arranged numerically the instructions may indicate that requests may be made by number only. A list that does not give enough bibliographical information to identify the item fully is a waste of time and effort.

Mailing lists of exchange partners should be exact and complete. The lists may be in sheet form, on cards, or on computer tapes or other mechanical devices, such as Addressograph plates. Flexibility in adding, deleting, or manipulating should be taken into consideration. In many cases the address used for any one exchange partner may vary according to what is being sent. The recipient may wish all correspondence sent to one address, all books sent to another, and serials sent to still another (or several others depending on subject matter).

A very useful item for the gift and exchange unit is a supply of preprinted, self-addressed labels. These can be enclosed with any correspondence that will bring a reply in package form. This is not only a convenience for the sender, but it also ensures delivery to the right place and probably to the attention of the right person. If the labels are printed on a distinctive colored paper, they are less likely to be lost by the respondent and can be segregated easily in the mail room so as not to be confused with purchased materials. Such labels also alert the gift and exchange staff to the fact that there has been previous correspondence, which should be matched with the package. After all, how could the sender use such a label unless it had been sent (or given) in some kind of communication?

THE ECONOMICS OF EXCHANGE

There is an old dictum that says, "No one gets anything for nothing," and an exchange division is no exception to that rule.[3] A wisely run and efficient exchange setup may well pay off in dividends, but a capital investment is necessary to produce these dividends.

The economics of exchange have not been thoroughly studied, and certainly they should be. Many libraries have discarded the idea of an exchange program as being uneconomical. As a matter of fact, this decision seems to be based mainly on guesswork, since actual costs and value of return figures are not available in great depth.[4] Actually, it would be difficult to assess the value of an exchange program except over a period of years, for so often an exchange arrangement can be likened to an investment in the stock market: you invest now with a view to long-range gain. For 500 items sent out this year a library might receive in return only 250. However, two years from now that same number of items sent might bring back 1,000 or 1,500 items in return.

Roughly, the expenses of exchange can be divided into two groups: the obvious and the hidden. In the obvious column are such expenses as personnel, equipment, stationery, packing materials, mailing costs, and costs of exchange materials. Depending on the size of the organization, of course, the amount these factors involve will vary considerably.

Now to the hidden costs of an exchange program. In the matter of obtaining materials for exchange—and I am speaking now of materials "hot off the press," current exchange items as opposed to duplicates and discards—when a library obtains exchange materials from the university press or some other outside source by gift or allotment, who pays? Certainly these items are not a gift from the gods, and if the cost doesn't come directly from the library budget, some other source must meet the expense. Another item, often forgotten, is office space and overhead.

Concerning the exchange of duplicates, thought must be given to the expense of carrying on this activity. A great many libraries reproduce lists of materials for exchange. These lists are then sent to the libraries on their exchange roster. Such a procedure can be quite costly in the clerical time required for sorting, listing, reproducing the list, and mailing. An average list may contain from 250 to 500 titles or listings. If a typist can list these at the rate of forty-five per hour and is paid at the rate of three dollars an hour, the cost of preparing such a list would be eighteen to thirty-three dollars for just the listing. Add to this the cost of arranging entries alphabetically (or in any other way), reproducing the list, addressing and mailing, postage, selecting, and wrapping and mailing the materials requested. And this whole procedure may be repeated as frequently as once a month. At the other end of the process is the time required in checking incoming lists and issuing requesting letters.

Considering this costly procedure many librarians have concluded that exchange generally doesn't pay. It is cheaper to sell to dealers whatever they will take at whatever price they will pay and pulp the rest. Some libraries have come to the realization that to list items of which there is only one copy is much too costly, but to list items of which there are ten or more copies is to spread the listing cost over that many copies. More practical, perhaps, is the process of sending and receiving want lists, especially for periodicals. One might appropriately request back issues or runs of periodicals on exchange from their issuing institutions or at least from other institutions in the same country. Ordinarily, daily, weekly, or biweekly publications or ephemera would not be available in this way; a better source for these would be the Universal Serials and Book Exchange (see p. 21), or a commercial dealer. Scholarly journals are more likely to be available from exchange partners than would trade publications. All this assumes, of course, that available materials are arranged for easy accessibility.

Speaking of duplicate materials, presumably in single copies, there is the question of storage. Fremont Rider pointed out that "all cost accounting studies confirm that to store a book today in a conventional standard book stack costs approximately fifteen cents a volume a year. To store one average size library book requires today directly or indirectly a three dollar investment in book storage."[5] And that was in 1950! Presumably, of course, exchange materials will not be stored for a year or even a major portion of it, but let us assume that 500 books are stored for a period of three months while the list is being made up and circulated and the materials finally distributed. That cost is something to consider.

On the credit side of the exchange program is the value, itself hard to estimate, of the materials received on exchange. Since many such publications are not otherwise available either as gifts or through commercial channels there is no easy way to discover their value. As Kipp has pointed out:

A library normally finds it expensive to locate foreign titles needed, and additionally expensive to locate the bibliographic data needed for ordering through commercial channels. These steps are all the more expensive when material needed is from a country where publications are not systematically listed. The need for such data is often eliminated through the use of exchange, for a foreign institution then supplies on exchange either particular types of publications or all of its publications as they are published. Placing costs aside, many titles would be almost impossible to locate except through exchange.[6]

It will be seen that although the function of an exchange division is to acquire books and other library materials without direct purchase, the division still needs funds to operate.

COOPERATIVE EXCHANGE EFFORTS

Several specialized groups of libraries in this country have set up cooperative programs for the exchange of duplicate materials among their membership. Perhaps the oldest of these programs is that carried on among the medical or health science libraries. Following is a statement issued by the Medical Library Association, Inc., in April 1978:

More than one-third of a million titles change hands annually among the institutional members of the Medical Library Association who participate in the MLA Exchange Program. This service, which has been in existence since 1898, relocated materials to where they are needed for the cost of postage only. Today, more than 1,260 health sciences libraries which are MLA institutional members rely on the exchange to build their collections and fill gaps in journal runs.

A member library submits a list of its duplicate journal titles, and each list includes the name and address of the library offering material. These lists are assembled at MLA Headquarters and distributed to all institutional members. More than 10,000 duplicate journals are listed in each monthly Exchange. Participating libraries check the material needed on the lists and send requests directly to the donor library. When the materials are received by the requesting library, shipping costs are refunded to the donor library.

Another such exchange program is maintained by the American Theological Library Association. In a letter to this author, dated April 24, 1978, the executive director outlined their operation in this way:

A periodical exchange program has been carried out among institutional member schools of ATLA since as early as 1953. At its latest annual conference (June 1977) the association voted to change the name of its program to Library Materials Exchange to reflect more accurately the current nature of the endeavor. Books as well as periodicals are frequently offered. In addition to holding institutional membership in ATLA (regular or interim, another 1977 innovation to allow for collection upbuilding by unaccredited schools through the exchange program) participants agree to circulate lists of their own duplicate materials and to supply items from that list as requested. Postage is reimbursed only if it exceeds fifty cents per shipment.

The exchange program chairperson annually distributes lists of institutions participating in the program. This past year lists were distributed as pressure-sensitive, computer printed labels to facilitate mailing of the duplicate listings. Institutions that have not provided a list in the past 18 months are removed from the program.

The Committee on the Exchange of Duplicates of the American Association of Law Libraries oversees a program of exchanging legal periodicals, federal (U.S.) administrative agency decisions, and subject case reports (privately published). Their invitation to join the 1977-78 exchange reads in part as follows:

The purpose of the Committee is to encourage the exchange of duplicate materials among law libraries, by issuing periodic lists of exchange materials available from member libraries and to study and recommend to the Association from time to time methods to facilitate exchanges.

Libraries that wish to join in the Exchange should send $15.00 as dues to the Chairperson of the Committee. Dues are to be paid in the form of a subscription to the Exchange lists, as some libraries have found it difficult to acquire funding for items classified as memberships. The dues are renewed annually. When the Chairperson receives your dues, you will at that time be assigned a code number, if one has not been assigned to your library, to be used on this year's lists and all future lists. . . .

During the past four years (1973-77) the following types of material have been offered for exchange through the Committee:

1973-74: Legal Texts and Treatises
1974-75: Legal Periodicals
1975-76: Legal Periodicals. State and Provincial Case & Attorney General Reports.

1976-77:   Legal Periodicals. American Bar Association General and Section
            Publications.
Several weeks before the time for the compilation of a list, the chairperson
will send out to each participating library a reminder of the subject matter of
the list, the compiler, and the deadline for contributions.

Committee members volunteer to produce the lists, and their institutions are reimbursed for printing, envelope, and postage costs incurred while doing one of these lists. The average cost for a typical
list is $375, hence the subscription fee of $15. Institutions preparing
a list are also exempt from paying the $15 fee. There are currently 189
member institutions in the Exchange program.

The Music Library Association has tried several times to set up a
workable exchange program. However, a letter to the author dated
April 25, 1978, from the president of the Association indicates: "Our
attempts in the past to establish a Committee on the Exchange of
Music Materials have not been successful, probably because most
music libraries, like other special collections, are subordinate parts
of larger institutions. Hence they normally do not carry on exchange
activities of their own."

The Universal Serials and Book Exchange, Inc., known as USBE,
occupies a unique place in the U.S. and international library scene.
Operating as the United States Book Exchange, Inc., from 1948 to
1975, USBE is an autonomous, nonprofit, self-supporting, cooperative venture, devised by librarians to absorb, refine, and redistribute
a valuable commodity that might otherwise be lost: the millions of
useful publications that the original owning institutions cannot put to
use in their own collections nor otherwise dispose of profitably. In
thirty years USBE has placed more than 13 million publications in
libraries from a total of approximately 50 million items handled.

USBE is governed by officers and a board of directors chosen in
annual elections by representatives in 40 sponsoring library associations and in more than 1600 member libraries. The latter pay an annual
membershp fee plus a standard handling fee for each publication
ordered and received from USBE; the total of these fees constitutes
USBE's sole income. Member libraries also pay shipping charges on
consignments they send to and receive from USBE.

Any kind of library (except those of individuals) is eligible for
USBE membership, as are most library organizations. Present members include libraries of national governments; those of universities
and other academic institutions; public libraries; and library net-

works and library associations. There are 1300 member institutions in the United States and 325 in fifty-five other countries, the largest number of these being in Canada.

The stocks of publications contributed by these institutions and others include 4 million items, of which 95 percent are periodicals and serials ranging from current issues back to early ones and 5 percent are books and government documents. There is a wide subject range. The majority of the publications are in English, but many other languages are represented. Most publications are in research areas.

Member libraries may select publications by several methods, choosing the methods most effective for their needs and processes. For periodical needs, USBE can process requests on 3-x-5-inch forms or want lists; for these USBE provides printed forms if needed. The receiving library pays a standard handling fee for each publication it orders and receives. Monthly lists from USBE provide members with information on available books, government documents, and periodicals at regular fees, plus journals at "bargain" prices, that is, prices less than the regular fees or at low rates for particularly valuable items. Interlibrary loan request forms are accepted and handled as regular orders at the standard handling fees. Nonmembers are welcome to request periodical issues from USBE at higher per-item fees.

USBE has maintained its operations over a thirty year period by providing libraries with several advantages: (1) a clearing house in which their surplus publications are received and made available to libraries; (2) a source of publications over a broad spectrum, including recent issues, out-of-print and in-print books and journals, back files, and many titles available from no other source; (3) fast service; and (4) economies effected through low cost and simplified methods.

BOOKS-ACROSS-THE-SEA

A very special kind of exchange program is that sponsored by the English-Speaking Union (E-SU).[7] Books-Across-The Sea (BAS) started during World War II, when the Outpost, a group of concerned Americans stationed in war-torn England, recognized the urgent need for American books. At their request, book-minded Americans sent seventy books speedily; the books were welcomed as ambassadors, and seventy books were shipped in exchange from London. Thus began an exchange designed to reflect the life and culture of each country. This exchange now reaches out to Australia, New Zealand, Canada, and India. The Books-Across-The-Sea library at the English-

Speaking Union's national headquarters in New York, which began from an initial collection of seventy books, now boasts over 8,500 volumes—primarily of books from the Commonwealth. Over the years a unique research collection has been made available to E-SU members as well as to a wider public in search of information.

The BAS staff and expert panel members constantly watch for early announcements of forthcoming books that will be appropriate to send to Commonwealth countries. Books that present American life and culture in the humanities and social sciences and children's books are especially considered. Religion, sciences, and textbooks are not sent. Very popular titles apt to be published simultaneously in England are not considered. The unusual titles, the books likely to be missed are sought. At times, especially with children's books, the typography or the illustrator will cause the book to be chosen even if the subject does not directly relate to American life and culture.

Publishers' catalogs and *Publisher's Weekly* announcement numbers furnish the first clues. As soon as a title is deemed important, a request for a review copy is sent to the publisher. A card is made for the title and that card records all information about the particular book: place and date of reviews, price and publisher, the place to which the panel decides to send the review copy if selected, the reason for rejection, and the annotation to be used for the lists of books sent.

As later reviews appear in *Kirkus Reviews, Library Journal, School Library Journal,* and other review media, they are noted on the control card and help to decide if the title should be included on the pre-selection list to be sent to panel members. Even later, *The Horn Book* and *New York Times* Sunday and daily reviews are consulted, and books that were missed at the time of the first announcement are requested from publishers.

Quarterly, each selection panel—adults' and children's—receives a selection list of some seventy-five to a hundred titles that may be important to send to the Commonwealth countries. The panelists, all deeply involved in books—librarians, editors, professors, authors, child study specialists—and all with the background that produces "a nose for books," meet and in free discussion eliminate some titles, add others, and end with about 90 percent of the books approved for listing and sending abroad. Certain books, because of style, format, importance of the topic and its treatment, and general appeal are considered outstanding and are designated "ambassadors." Extra copies of these books are requested from the publishers so that every country in the exchange may have a copy.

An annotated list of all the books selected is prepared and sent to the regular mailing list, to all exchange countries, and to all publishers whose books are included on the list. How can one book spread its influence through five widely separated countries?

It would be pleasant to send a copy of each title selected to each country. However, at the last adult panel meeting, a hundred titles were available for final selection; seventy-eight were chosen. It would not be feasible to ask the publishers of the seventy-eight for four additional copies of each title. Replies from the four publishers whose books were chosen as being especially representative indicated that they considered it an honor, and they were very cooperative in providing extra copies.

Annotated lists are used as the vehicle for spreading the word to all the countries in the exchange. These lists are duplicated here and abroad. They are distributed to anyone requesting them. The lists are on hand at important meetings and exhibitions. In the United States, the lists of U.S. books sent abroad and the lists of books received from abroad are distributed to hundreds of organizations and individuals who have requested that their names be on the mailing list. Public and school libraries use the lists to purchase books for their collections; publishers are delighted to know that their books are receiving global recognition; and members use them to obtain the books from their local libraries or book stores.

The same process is used by the other countries in the exchange. Books are selected, lists annotated, and books shipped to the exchange countries. In the United States, however, the Commonwealth books are available at the BAS library for members to borrow when books are not on loan to schools and libraries. The Los Angeles County Public Library, for instance, had 333 books for exhibition and circulation for a three-month period.

NOTES

1. Herbert A. Keller, "Memoranda on Library Cooperation," no. 1 (Washington, D.C.: n.p., 1941), p. 10.

2. Alfred H. Lane, "Exchange Materials Used in College and University Libraries," *College and Research Libraries* 8, no. 49 (January 1947).

3. This section is partly adapted from a paper presented by the author to the Acquisitions Round Table, American Library Association, New York City, July 2, 1952.

4. But see Ian W. Thom, "Duplicate Exchange: A Cost Analysis," *Library Resources & Technical Services* 1, no. 2 (Spring 1957): 81-84; and John E.

Galejs, "Economics of Serials Exchange," *Library Resources & Technical Services* 16, no. 4 (Fall 1972): 511-20.

5. Fremont Rider, "Microcard and the Cost of Book Storage," *Transactions of the Special Libraries Association,* 41st Annual Convention (1950): 9.

6. U.S., Interdepartmental Committee on Scientific and Cultural Cooperation, *The International Exchange of Publications,* prepared by Laurence J. Kipp (Wakefield, Mass.: Murray Printing Co., 1950), p. 31.

7. This section was adapted from a release issued by the Books-Across-The-Sea program of the English-Speaking Union and authored by Helen Wessells Hettinger.

ADDITIONAL REFERENCES

Carter, Harriet H. "Setting Up an Exchange Operation in the Small Special Library." *Library Resources & Technical Services* 22(Fall 1978):380-85.

Clayton, P. R. "Are Duplicate Lists Worthwhile?" *Australian Library Journal* 23(October 1974):321-22. This article explores time-cost statistics.

Collins, J. A. "The International Exchange Service." *Library Resources & Technical Services* 10, no. 3 (Summer 1966):337-41.

Eggleton, Richard. "The ALA Duplicates Exchange Union—A Study and Evaluation." *Library Resources & Technical Services* 19, no. 2 (Spring 1975):148-63.

Institute on the Acquisition of Foreign Materials. Compiled and edited by Theodore Samore. Metuchen, N.J.: Scarecrow Press, 1973, pp. 46-52.

Lupton, D. W. "Duplicate Periodical Problem in the Academic Library." *Library Resources & Technical Services* 20(Spring (1976):167-70. This is an analysis of the problem of periodical duplication.

United Nations Educational, Scientific and Cultural Organization. *Handbook on the International Exchange of Publications.* 3rd ed. Paris: UNESCO, 1964.

Vanwijngaerden, F. "Improving Exchange of Publications with Developing Countries in Africa: A Few Suggestions." *UNESCO Bulletin for Libraries* 30(March-April 1976):90-92.

Williams, Edwin E. "Exchanges: National and International." *Library Trends* 2(April 1954):562-72.

World of Learning, 1977-78. 28th ed. London: Europa, 1977.

4 | Gifts to Libraries

Gifts are a vital source of library materials, as the frequent mention of important gifts in library literature attests. Aside from large or famous collections or rare single volumes or manuscripts, the common "garden variety" materials also play a large role in the development and maintenance of collections. Where do they come from?

The sources of gifts are legion: the professor who is clearing out his office in preparation for retirement; the householder who is moving to another city; the former graduate who is running out of shelf space in his apartment; the bequest of a rare book collector; the author who wants to be sure his work is available for posterity; the corporation whose history should be preserved; the wealthy businessman who wants his generosity to be honored; the ordinary citizen who wants a tax deduction; the selfless soul who is truly interested in the development of the library's collections. These are merely examples of sources of unsolicited gifts which may turn up in a library on almost any day of the year.

There are also materials to be had without charge simply on request. Solicitation of gifts has become an important activity in many institutions. Don't be too proud to request gifts—the worst that can happen will be a refusal. After a little practice, compunctions will soon disappear. The key, as one librarian has said, is "boldness tempered by respectful courtesy." Publications like the *Bulletin* of the Public Affairs Information Service, *The Weekly Record,* published by *Publisher's Weekly,* the *UNESCO Bulletin for Libraries,* and the *Vertical File Service* all list free materials. Frequently, too, journals in special subject fields mention items available for the asking. *Library Journal, American Libraries, Wilson Bulletin,* and *College & Research Libraries* are examples of these. In addition, membership in professional organizations sometimes brings free items. The U.S. government (and other governments, too) is a prime source of "freebies." Witness the publications listed in U.S. Superintendent of Documents, *Selected U.S. Government Documents,* or the commercial publication by Norback, Graig and Peter, *Everything You Can Get from the Government Free . . . or Almost Free* (New York: Van Nostrand, 1975). In addition, there is the series of *Educators Guides to: Free Films, Free Filmstrips, Free Guidance Materials, Free Health, Physical Education and Recreation Materials, Free Social Studies Materials, Free Teaching Aids,* and *Educators Index of Free Materials.* Paperback racks constantly display books listing free materials. Newspapers and popular magazines sometimes mention available publications in their news stories. The alert librarian is aware of these sources and takes advantage of them.

There seems to be a direct correlation between the size and importance of a library and the number of gift items it attracts. The *Annual Report of the Librarian of Congress* for the year 1975 indicates that receipts by gift for that report year totaled 1,625,401 items. In the same period of time the Columbia University Libraries received 49,795 items, exclusive of journals received on a regular basis, as gifts; the New York Public Library recorded "several thousand individuals," corporations, foundations, and estates as donors that year.

Memorial gifts have become popular in recent years. Gifts of books or the money to buy them are presented as memorials to friends or relatives or even to honor living persons. However, the costs attendant upon a program of memorial gifts should be given considerable thought. Usually such memorials involve special bookplates, individual handling, and special correspondence to thank the donors and to notify relatives, heirs, or honorees. Personnel costs may outweigh the value of the gift, although it might be politic, in some cases, to absorb the extra cost without murmur. There must, of course, be agreement between the library and the donor on the acceptability of the particular title or titles selected.

Endowments, trust funds, annuities, insurances, bequests, and deferred gifts are other sources of library gifts. Most academic institutions are prepared to provide information to those in a position to advise on these matters, such as bankers, doctors, lawyers, ministers, and accountants. For potential donors who wish to include a library in their wills, most major libraries (or their parent institutions) have prepared leaflets to explain how this should be done and showing the correct corporate designation of the library as well as several possible forms of devises and bequests. Columbia University prefaces its folder with this message:

The purpose of this leaflet is to assist those friends of Columbia who wish to include some gift to the University in their Wills. It gives the correct corporate designation of the University, which should be used, and suggests several forms of devises and bequests which could be considered by the maker of the Will in consultation with the attorney who should prepare it.

The body of the leaflet is shown below.

♛ I GIVE* AND BEQUEATH TO THE TRUSTEES OF COLUMBIA UNIVERSITY IN THE CITY OF NEW YORK . . . .

	the sum of_____Dollars,
or	_____shares of the capital stock of_____ Corporation,
or	the following described property_____,

and

IF YOU WISH:

to make the bequest unrestricted, add:	to be used for the University's general purposes.

but

. . . . to express a preference that the gift be used for a particular school, then instead add:	Without imposing any restrictions upon this bequest, I request it be used for the School of_____.

or

. . . . to be still more specific in your preference with respect to the gift, then instead add:	Without imposing any restrictions upon this bequest, I request it be used (e.g.) to assist worthy students.

but

. . . . to actually restrict the use of the gift, add *either:*	to be used (e.g.) to aid worthy students in (Columbia College, School of Engineering, Graduate School of Business).

or

words to express such other specific purposes as may be desired, such as:	to be used to buy books for the Law School.

but

. . . . to require that the principal of the bequest remain intact, restricting the use of the fund to income alone, then add:	to be held, invested, and reinvested and the net income therefrom used (e.g.) to aid worthy students in the College of Physicians and Surgeons.

*If any of the property is real estate, include the word DEVISE after GIVE

ACCEPTABILITY OF GIFTS

An established library cannot afford to accept everything that is offered as a gift. If the subject matter of the gift does not fit within the collecting policy of the library, it would be folly to accept the gift. It is almost inconceivable, for instance, that the library of a theological seminary would have any use for a collection of books on thermodynamics. It is also unlikely that such an offer would be made, however.

A library probably should not accept a gift when almost certainly 90 percent of the material would duplicate present holdings. The cost of processing such a gift would be prohibitive considering the small useful portion of the collection. But even here caution should be exercised.

There comes to mind the story of a bequest to a large university library of all or any portion of a collection of books that had been in the family of the deceased for two or three generations. When the cartons and barrels of the books were cursorily examined in a warehouse previous to taking possession, the first impression was that here was a typical gentleman's library of the late nineteenth and early twentieth centuries. The books were those that almost any library would already have: sets of Scott, Thackeray, and Hardy, individual novels of the period, a few travel books, and the like. It was decided, however, that since the books were in excellent condition and many of them could be used for replacements or added copies, the library would accept the total collection. Later, in a more careful examination, it was discovered that the gift contained many first editions, some rare volumes, and one unique book which was worth all the time and expense of processing. What looked like an ordinary copy of Dickens's *A Christmas Carol* turned out to have a full-page hand-written note on the flyleaf inscribed to a young boy and signed Charles Dickens.

There are further considerations to be kept in mind when accepting a gift. When asked about leaving (or giving) books, money, real estate, securities, or other property to the library, the librarian would do well to consider that the fewer the restrictions the better for the library. When a donor leaves money for a special collection of books in his honor and decrees that these books shall not circulate, shall be housed in a special area, and shall be cataloged and maintained in specific ways, the library in future years may find itself saddled with an intolerable burden. If, however, a bequest or gift has terminal strings, the bequest or gift may be much more welcome. For instance, an author or famous person who gives his manuscripts with the proviso

Like a real Christmas gift, this rare first edition of Dickens' tale of Old Scrooge and Tiny Tim came to the Columbia University Libraries as a complete surprise in a collection bequeathed by Miss Hilda Ward. Making it almost priceless is the flyleaf inscription, written by Charles Dickens himself when he gave the volume to an English boy, Frank Powell of Peckham over 100 years ago. In 1850 this inscribed copy was given to an American girl, Miss Ward's grandmother, and it remained unknown to bibliographers until it came to light among the books in Miss Ward's bequest. Reprinted from the *Columbia Alumni News,* December 1951. (See also Frontispiece.)

that they may not be made available to the public (that is, the library's constituency) until five years after the donor's death is not placing an undue burden on the library. It merely means proper care and storage for a period of time after which the restriction is removed. This kind of restriction is frequently placed on the reminiscences gained through oral history projects which many libraries have recently inaugurated.

Thought should be given to the processing costs entailed in the acceptance of a gift. This is especially true of serials, since the initial cataloging is only the beginning; additional costs are incurred as more issues come in and additional volumes are bound. As for books, if most of the useful materials in a gift will have to be rebound, or if additional personnel will be needed to sort, search, and catalog the collection within a certain time limit, it might be better to turn down the offer. One consistent (and considerate) donor to the Columbia University Libraries gave only one or two French books at a time, but he also gave money to have the books bound.

There is also the cost of cataloging the books. Figures will vary from place to place and from time to time, but currently, at one large academic library, it costs approximately $12 to catalog a book for the first time and as much as $3.67 per title to add a copy for a departmental library. Shared cataloging and computerized availability of catalog records are bringing these costs down. The MARC (machine readable cataloging) tapes issued by the Library of Congress are a good example of such innovations. So, too, is CIP (cataloging in publication), which appears on the verso of the title page of most current U.S. publications.

Backlogs and storage problems frequently plague the library. Gifts tend to come not in a steady flow but in spurts. One week may produce 250 books, and the next week may bring 20,000 volumes. Coping with this flow is not always easy. Space and personnel—or, rather, the lack of them—are the chief bugaboos. Seasons of the year seem to have some influence: at the end of the academic year when professors retire, in the fall when people tend to change residences, in the spring when people clean house, in the winter between semesters when new faculty arrive and displace others from their office space, and just before the end of the year when taxes are looming there seems to be no let-up.

However, the fact that a gift offer has certain conditions attached to it should not be automatic cause for turning down the gift. The Columbia University Libraries were recently offered a 20,000-volume library which represented the life-long collection of a professor of sociology who might well be described as a Renaissance scholar. The quality and scope of the collection were remarkable. The professor's widow, who offered the collection, wanted to be sure that all the items in the collection would be made available to other scholars, that each would carry an appropriate bookplate, that none of the books would be sold, and that any titles not needed or wanted by Columbia would be offered to a university library (specifically named) in Africa. She wanted to know where each book could be found if anyone asked. This involved listing each of the books and identifying its location, a tremendous, time-consuming task with its attendant personnel costs. This was further complicated by the fact that these volumes had to be segregated from all other acquisitions until each had been identified and its location known.

But, thanks to today's technology, it was felt that this burden would be acceptable, considering the value of the collection. After first removing over 700 volumes, which were added to the Rare Book and Manuscript Library, selection of several thousand volumes for use in the general collections began. These were put into the computer listing of materials in process, showing the destination library for each title and identifying each as to source. Thus, a computer print-out of all titles from this collection could be extracted later. All titles not needed by Columbia were recorded in a special computer list and given a numerical location number. This provided bibliographic control of the total collection.

Speaking of restrictions, depository collections should also be watched carefully. The U.S. Depository Library system provides designated libraries throughout the country with the publications of the federal government on a selective basis so that the total populace will have access to these materials. The terms of acceptance are usually not hard to meet. But there are other kinds of depositories: from government organizations (for example, state document depositories), from businesses (such as The James F. Lincoln Arc Welding Foundation Library), and even from individuals. Here are some factors to consider before accepting depository collections. Are there limitations in the use of the materials? How much will it cost to handle the materials? Are there time limits on the collection, that is, must the library keep the materials a specific length of time or is the use of the materials restricted for a period of time? Are there conditions on who may or may not use the materials? How much space will the materials require? All of these factors (and perhaps others as well) should be spelled out in a written agreement.

It is important that the donor is aware of what is going to happen to the books he gives: that some will be cataloged and added to the library's collections; that some may be discarded for poor physical condition or because they are superseded editions; and that others may be sold, exchanged, or given away. The widow of a collector of chess books presented the collection to a university library and was not told at the time of the gift how the collection would be handled. As it happened, some of the books were sold to dealers, one of whom discovered the name of the original owner. He approached the widow and offered to buy any other chess volumes she might still have. The donor, understandably, was outraged and demanded that the university buy back all the books it had sold, de-catalog the ones it intended to keep, and ship the total collection to another institution. The cost, not only in financial terms but in embarrassment and poor public relations, could have been avoided if the library's procedures had been explained at the outset. As a corollary, don't promise what can't be delivered.

Rejecting a gift is not always an easy thing to do. It is a good idea, therefore, to suggest an alternative to the prospective donor; another library, perhaps, or a book drive, a local charity, or an organization that sends books to underdeveloped countries. The Asia Foundation in San Francisco is one example of such an organization. The philosophy behind this is twofold: to maintain tact and good will and to ensure that a later offer of more acceptable materials may be made.

ESTIMATES AND APPRAISALS

One of the most controversial subjects in the area of gifts to libraries is the matter of evaluations for estate, insurance, or income tax purposes. It is likely that everyone accepts the philosophy behind the statement on appraisal of gifts as formulated by the Committee on Manuscript Collections of the Rare Books and Manuscripts Section of the Association of College and Research Libraries (see Appendix C), but it is not always easy to live up to. There is a fast-growing awareness that gifts given to libraries are tax deductible; and with the tax burden as it is today, most people are anxious to make the most of this, and no one can blame them for wanting to do so.

It is unwise for a library to make its own appraisals for the use of donors. In the first place, the appraisal may be thrown out by the tax courts on the basis that the appraisal was made by an interested party. In addition, a library-given appraisal or evaluation implies that the library (corporately) or a member or members of its staff can reasonably back up such appraisals of similar materials. If the material is worth appraising, a competent appraiser should be called in from the outside. It is possible that the cost of the appraisal will be borne by the donor. The Internal Revenue Service recommends that the donor pay for this service. (Rates currently charged by appraisers run roughly between $50 and $200 an hour plus expenses.) The costs of such appraisals are also tax deductible as a miscellaneous deduction.

However, calling in an appraiser for every request is just not feasible. (Gifts of property valued at $200 or less do not need to be appraised. See Appendix A.) It could very well be that the cost would exceed the value of the materials. What to do, then, to avoid annoying a donor (or losing a gift)? The library might well provide an estimate of value based on available evidence—listings in dealers' catalogs, book auction records, quoted subscription prices, list prices of books still in print, and so on. In a case like this, the basis for the evaluation should always be stated, perhaps using such hedging words as "estimate" and "approximately." However, it should be pointed out that such an estimate is just that—it is not an appraisal. The responsibility for documenting a claim for deduction rests with the donor. One librarian gets around this by writing the donor a letter to the effect that although he cannot make an appraisal, he would have been willing to pay X number of dollars for this collection (or item) if it had appeared in the open market.

Two current practices of which the librarian should be aware (but not responsible) are the taking of tax deductions for books and other materials received as review copies (here the donor has paid no money out of pocket and has had the use of the books, yet claims a deduction), and taking a double deduction: once for money expended as a "professional expense" and once again when giving the books to the library.

A statement of value by a competent appraiser should be a document (sometimes the donor requests that it be notarized) outlining the competency of the appraiser, the basis on which the appraisal was arrived at, and the date and for whom the appraisal was made. Each of the first three of the following sample of letters of appraisal illustrates a different type of gift, but each has a personal note about it reflecting the fact that the appraiser has actually spent time considering all facets of the gifts and their usefulness to the recipient library.

SAMPLE LETTER OF APPRAISAL—1

Dear _____,

I have examined your fine file of unbound volumes of scientific periodicals as listed below. The sets are most unusual in that their condition is nearly pristine and the collection is of long and unbroken runs.

Bulletin, American Association of Petroleum Geologists.
Vols. 13-62, 1920-date. 49 vols. $ 750.
Evolution. Vols. 1-30, 1947-76. 30 vols.   350.
Journal of Paleontology. Vols. 1-52, 1927-78. 52 vols.   1500.
Paleontology. Vols. 3-19, 1960-76. 16 vols.   300.
Systematic Zoology. Vols. 5-26, 1960-77. 21 vols.   300.

The total worth of this unusual collection is $32,000, a figure representative of a fair price in today's antiquarian market in any transaction between a willing seller and a willing buyer.

Please call on me if I can be of further use to you.

Cordially,

SAMPLE LETTER OF APPRAISAL—2

Dear_____,

It has been a pleasure for me to learn about the four interesting book collections you have given to the_____College,_____University and State College libraries in 1977. Gifts of this kind are always appreciated and useful to such institutions (as your letters of acknowledgment signify); and when they are so well distributed to where they will be most useful, the gifts are enhanced in value so much more.

In brief, the collections which I have appraised are as follows:

(1)   _____University Library—6 items, as described in your accompanying letter of acknowledgment. These I have appraised at the following valuation: Lankes' woodblock (1936), $65; Fendrick Gallery catalogues (1976, 1977), $5; Blake's Pencil Drawings (1927), $125; Johnson's Romantic Legend (1977), $35; Partridge, Original Issue of "The Spectator" (1939), $100; and Ezra Pound's *Quia Pauper Amavi* (1919), $200.

Total $530.00

(2)   _____Rare Book and Manuscript Library, _____University— A remarkable collection of some 50 books used by Paul Horgan as source material in preparation for writing [title]. These research pieces all have [author's] bookplate and many of them have his annotations and notes of reference, which are of considerable interest to students of [author] and of the history of the American southwest.

Total $695.00

(3)   Division of Library Science Library, _____State College—The collection of about 50 reference books, children's literature, and children's books illustrated by important artists makes a fine addition to the study and reference resources of [the State's] only library school. The greatest strength in this collection lies in the scarce and unusual illustrated books which will be of use to the students in the arts as well as in the library school.

Total $760.00

(4)   _____Library (Main Library), _____State College—A collection of 85 miscellaneous books, principally in the fields of history, literature, art, and biography. The books range in value from $2 to one of $50 (most $3-5). As the Librarian's acknowledgment attests, they are welcome additions to the college's general collections.

Total $486.00

Thus in the aggregate, I appraise those four collections at a total sum of $2,471.00, a value that would be acceptable for sale by a willing seller to a willing buyer in today's antiquarian market.

Please let me know if I can be of use to you at any time.

Cordially,

P.S.   For the file record that you may wish to keep concerning my qualifications the following should suffice, but please let me know if additional information is required.

I am a professional librarian with nearly fifty years of experience in the administration of academic and special libraries, as well as in the antiquarian book trade. My regular clients for appraisal include The American Museum of Natural History (where I also serve as Collection Development Consultant to the Library), The University of Rhode Island Libraries, Brown University Special Collections Library, New York Academy of Medicine, Downstate Medical Research Library, Yale University Historical Medicine Library, etc., etc. In the past two years I have been called to appraise collections for the American Philosophical Society Library, Dickinson College Library, Duke University, Harvard University, etc. I am past chairman of the American Library Association/Association of College and Research Libraries Section on Rare Books & Manuscripts, and have compiled all editions of the standard reference book, *Subject Collections: A Guide to Special Collections* (4th edition, 1974).

SAMPLE LETTER OF APPRAISAL—3

Dear _____,

It was a very pleasant experience to have had an opportunity to examine your family's autograph album (the one bound in red niger-morocco, untitled, with a golden griffin or wyvern stamped in the upper-left corner of the front cover, decorated with gilt floral inner dentelles in green niger-morocco panels, unsigned; also with embroidered floral fly-leaves, in the French style; the whole in a fitted black russion-morocco open-ended slipcase stamped "_____, 36 rue du Mont-Thapor, Paris").

I was quite unprepared for the wide range of original autographs and inscriptions (dated) from 1885 to 1949 in this one volume. There are, altogether, about 150 fine signatures, mostly one to a page, many with special personal inscriptions or quotations; there are also many others by important or famous artists who have signed drawings or sketches in these pages—a few in colors.

I have studied the collection by grouping the signatures into lists of classes of occupation: Literature (more than 50); Artists & Illustrators (over 30); Theatre personalities—actors, actresses, playwrights, producers, critics (some 35); Statesmen, Royalty, Nobility & Military (about 20); and Musicians and Vocalists (10); there are about five signatures I cannot decipher or otherwise identify without further research.

Among the Literati (more than 50), we have—as a brief sampling— G. K. Chesterton, Frank Stockton, Matthew Arnold, Rudyard Kipling, Hall Caine, Edward Everett Hale, James Lane Allen, Owen Wister, Lew Wallace, J. G. Whittier, Oliver Wendell Holmes, John Burroughs, John Hay, Mark Twain, Oliver Herford, Helen Keller & Annie Sullivan Macy, etc.

The Artists & Illustrators (over 30) are partially represented by the following, almost all of whom have added a page-size drawing which they have signed: Edwin Abbey, Elihu Vedder, Thomas Nast, Albert Sterner, Frank Myrick, Howard Pyle, Reginald Bathurst Birch, Frederick Remington, A. B. Frost, Villaneuve, Charles Dana Gibson, John Singer Sargent, J. Alden Weir, Sir Laurence Alma-Tadems, Rodin, etc.

Theatre personalities (some 35), many with inscriptions as well as signatures, include Edwin Booth, Sir Henry Irving, Joseph Jefferson, Ellen Terry, Helena Modjeska, Tomaso Salvini, Madge Kendal, Ada Rehan, William Winter, Ethel Barrymore, John Drew, Arthur Pinero, Eleanora Duse, Katherine Cornell, Noel Coward, Alfred

Lunt & Lynn Fontanne, etc.

Statesmen, Royalty, Nobility, & Military (about 20) are represented by Ulysses S. Grant, Theodore Roosevelt, and a third President of the United States—Dwight D. Eisenhower (who, we are told, was very impressed by an opportunity to sign on a facing page inscribed by William Tecumseh Sherman), Fridtjoff Nansen, Alexandra & Albert Edward—one page with other members of the Royal Family, Edward, George, Louise, Victoria, and Maude—George, King of the Hellenes, Constantine Duke of Sparta, etc.

The Musicians and Vocalists are fewer in number (10) but include such famous figures as Nellie Melba, Clara Louise Kelloge, Adelina Patti, and Jascha Heifitz.

Loosely laid into the album is a White House pass signed on the obverse by Eleanore Roosevelt; also, an unsigned self-caricature pen sketch by Alexander Woolcott.

Although autograph albums of this kind represent a genre of collecting that was not unusual at the turn of the century, it is most remarkable to find one with so many inscriptions with associative qualities so cordially humorous and relative to the person to whom they are dedicated. What could be more fun than a few bars of music transcribed and signed by Heifitz, or typical drawings by Frost, Nast, Remington, and Pyle? And how appropriate, since both Guy Wetmore Carryl and his father, Charles, are still remembered as outstanding humorists in the tradition of American literature, as modern reference books recall.

Added to these "association" factors, the appropriateness of the book as a gift to the _____ Memorial Library of _____ is extraordinary since many of the inscriptions are signed and dated by famous members or visitors to that historic American club. This is, indeed, a fine addition to the resources of the Library's outstanding collection of theatrical and literary memorabilia.

As a result of my careful examination of this album, as an expert and appraiser of literary materials, and in view of the considerations listed in the previous paragraphs, I consider this volume of original signatures, inscriptions, and illustrations to be worth $1750, representative of a fair price if offered by a willing seller to a willing buyer in today's antiquarian market.

Thank you for the opportunity to see this unique album, and congratulations on your intention to give it a home in the _____ Memorial Library of _____ where it will be preserved, appreciated, enjoyed, and useful to researchers.

Cordially,

SAMPLE LETTER OF APPRAISAL—4

To whom it may concern:

For some forty-five years I have been engaged in the buying, selling, and appraising of books and other printed and written materials. During that period I have appraised many collections for university and other libraries, and private individuals.

On September 11, 1978, at the Avery Library of Columbia University, I examined a small collection of books and pamphlets being donated to the Library by Mrs. _____. There are about thirty pieces in this collection, mainly in English but a few in German, and they are almost entirely on Art and on Architecture. Most of them are substantial works in fine condition, are recent, and in cloth binding; of the few that are in paper binding, some are also substantial works which will be useful to the library.

In my considered opinion, a fair and reasonable valuation of this collection is Three Hundred Forty Dollars ($340.00).

(signed)

Member Antiquarian Booksellers Association of America
Member Appraisers Association of America

Sometimes potential donors will make a temporary deposit of materials they intend to give at a later date, perhaps at a time more personally appropriate for a tax deduction. At that time, the donor should send the library a formal letter of gift.

From time to time legal questions arise in the handling of gifts. One such question is the legal definition of a book. Several years ago a major library received as a bequest a rather large and important collection with one string attached. Quoting in part from the will:

I give and bequeath to my son, _____, if he survives me, the choice of such five hundred (500) books in my library as he may select, and after my son has made such selection, I give and bequeath to _____ [library] such of the remaining books in my library as it may wish to accept. For the purpose of this Codicil to my will, my *Encyclopedia Britannica,* my bibliographies and other catalogues are each to be considered as one book.

This posed quite a problem in that the son interpreted each listing on the official appraisal as one book, regardless of how many titles or volumes were involved in the entry, and he also thought of any set or series of volumes (regardless of titles) as one book. In the effort to resolve this difficulty no one could find a legal definition of a book—and, as far as is known, no such definition has yet been found. In other words, is a book a physical volume or is it a title (regardless of the number of volumes)? And if a title is a book, which title do you count? The publisher's title of "The Collected Works of Washington Irving" may consist of twenty-five volumes, each with its own specific title. Is this to be counted as one book or twenty-five?

RECORDS OF GIFTS

It should be obvious even to the uninitiated that certain records of gifts must be created and kept. Vital information to be gathered would include the name and address of the donor, the date of the gift, the size of the gift (a count or estimate of the number of volumes), any conditions imposed on the acceptance (for example, to be book-plated in memory of someone, restraints on who may have access to the collection, time limit before it becomes available for use), the date of acknowledgment, the value if appraised or estimated internally, and a description of the collection either with a phrase or two or in detail.

These records should be kept indefinitely, at least for gifts from individuals. Records for gifts from corporate bodies—unless they are of major importance—may usually be weeded after a few years. Gift records are frequently referred to. It may happen that a donor, who claims to have given the library a book of her poetry a few years earlier, does not see it in the card catalog. A record of gifts allows the librarian to show the donor that the book was received and acknowledged. To explain why it doesn't appear in the catalog is another problem, especially if it was discarded as not being worthy of a place in the library's collection. In another case, a person may say that his mother-in-law gave some books to the library in the mid-1950s, and he would like to know if these included the family Bible, which he has been unable to locate. Could the library tell him? (This does not imply that the library must keep a complete list of all titles received as gifts.) More frequently a previous gift record is used to add another recent gift.

The easiest form for recording gifts is a 3-x-5-inch card on which most of the above-mentioned information can be stored. The cards are filed alphabetically by the donor's name. These can be kept in a relatively small file covering only the current year. After statistics for the year have been compiled, the cards can be interfiled in a master file which is a donor approach to former gifts.

As a supplement to the card file, a sheet record will be useful for large and important gifts. This form is used for a more detailed description of gifts than the description that can be entered on the gift card. This description is useful for publicity, for locating subject collections, and for identifying more quickly valuable gifts received during the year. To describe the gift more fully, a copy of the letter of appraisal can be filed with the form. These records are arranged by date of gift, thus giving a chronological approach to important gifts. At year's end these can be bound or kept in notebooks. A name index on cards provides another control for this record. This card file differs from the donor card record in that it lists names as subjects as well as names of donors. For instance, Richard Roe may give a collection of first editions of Robert Frost; both names would appear in the index. Or the gift of an oral history interview with Gerald Ford would probably contain hundreds of mentions of Henry Kissinger. Samples of gift records and forms appear in Appendix E.

It is probably a costly waste to list gifts item by item, especially since only a portion of all gifts finds a permanent place in the library's collection. An internal study at Columbia University Libraries several years ago showed that only 40 percent of all gifts received were actually incorporated into the library; the rest were dispersed in various ways. To list by author and title the 60 percent not kept in the library serves no useful purpose. (See chapter 5.)

GIFT POLICY STATEMENT

A statement of the library's policy on the acceptance and use of gifts is very desirable. Such a statement may be a set of guidelines for internal use by the library staff or it may take the form of a carefully worded brochure to be given to prospective donors. However, some librarians feel that such a publication may be too restrictive and not provide enough flexibility. In either case, the statement should include such topics as: (1) acceptability of gifts; (2) consideration of future as well as present needs; (3) restrictions on gifts; (4) guarantees in terms of cataloging, location, use, identification, care and housing, and acknowledgment; (5) legal title to gifts; (6) tax implications; and (7) gifts other than library materials (for example, money). An example of such a statement is that issued by the University of Utah library; it is reproduced in Appendix D. A quite different kind of statement, used by the Columbia University Libraries, is also shown.

As a corollary to the policy statement, a procedures manual is a "must" for the personnel who will be processing gifts (and exchanges).

This manual should describe in detail the step-by-step procedures in soliciting, receiving, recording, handling, and dispersing gifts to the library. This will necessarily be tailored to the local situation.

FRIENDS GROUPS

Groups known as Friends of the Library are very helpful as sources of gifts. Such groups are usually composed of both laymen and librarians whose common trait is an enthusiasm and interest in books and libraries. In addition to collecting and providing funds for special purchases for the library, they are often instrumental in securing gifts from individuals and organizations. The following article originally appeared in *College Library Notes For the College President* (no. 12, Summer 1971) and is reprinted here as an excellent exposition of the value of such groups.

A FRIENDS OF THE LIBRARY GROUP FOR MY COLLEGE?

by

Charles W. Mixer, Assistant Director of Libraries for Special Collections at Columbia University, and Secretary-Treasurer, Friends of the Columbia Libraries

The question indicated above could well be asked (in fact *should* be asked) by the college librarian and college president at any collegiate institution which has not as yet established a Friends group. The answer to the question may well turn out to be "yes"—not only for benefits that can accrue internally for the college but also because institutions are under some obligation to help in the locating and the preserving for scholarly use of rarities which are part of the nation's heritage.

The college and library officials may concede that the formation of a Friends group would theoretically be desirable, yet wonder whether the staff time and funds required to establish and to operate such a group could be justified. Such thoughts were, I know, very much in the minds of the library administrative staff and of some donors who were brought together in 1950 by Dr. Carl M. White, then the Director of Libraries at Columbia, to consider whether the Libraries should undertake the formation of a Friends association. (In the austere and even grave financial situation for academic institutions today in the early 1970s, the weighing of the pros and cons could understandably be prolonged.)

Actually once established, the Friends of the Library can be a most helpful ally: (1) The faculty members who join and the alumni and others in the community who join are apt to be or to have been frequent library users. This group, convinced of the library's usefulness, can be boosters of the best sort. (2) They can also serve a helpful liaison role in communicating information about library needs and services to other faculty members or to influential alumni or to others in the community. (3) They are the ones who, in the main, will enable the library to acquire for the collections the non-"bread and butter" items that will give the holdings scholarly importance and distinction. Such items may come as gifts from members' own holdings or by purchase with funds which they will have given for the purpose. (4) In the carrying out of the function mentioned immediately above they can perform a service of national importance to the scholarly world by bringing out from personal repository in homes, attics, basements, and even bank vaults into institutional care manuscripts, unique or rare books, and other research items. This will further the preservation of the latter and, assuming that the library sends bibliographic data about them to the National Union Catalog or the National Manuscript Catalog at the Library of Congress, will bring them into the main stream of resources for research—known to and accessible to scholars.

In connection with item (4) above, one sometimes finds unexpected strength and support among individual members of the Friends. A somewhat unusual case at Columbia, but one which gladdens the heart of the library administrator, is that of a person whose primary academic allegiance was to a distant university. He lived nearby and some years ago stopped in to see whether some correspondence and papers of George Santayana would be of interest as a gift. When the answer was in the affirmative, he began building our Santayana Collection, adding to it from time to time until today it is one of major importance. Later he made a similar inquiry about some John Masefield letters. The Masefield Collection which he started is modest in size as yet, but it is growing steadily through his interest. And now when the collection of a nationally renowned artist, book illustrator, and type designer was placed on the market, this same donor took the initiative (with library approval) in going to potential donors to seek gift funds and ultimately played the biggest role in raising the large amount needed for its purchase. The collection is now part of the holdings of the Libraries. The key point about this is that the all-important creative role with these three collections was played by a Friend of the Libraries whose first thought in terms of university aid would normally have been elsewhere.

Now if the college president and the college librarian have decided to go ahead with the formation of a Friends of the Library group, where will they obtain names of potential members? An important nucleus will be members of the faculty, particularly those in the humanities and the social sciences. Among those persons, library staff members can readily name some faculty members who are particularly avid users of the library. As suggested above, persons in the community who have important resources (book, manuscript or other) should be invited to join. Later, when the Friends group has been started, each member can be asked to submit the names of persons whom they would recommend for membership.

A useful device at an early period is to have an Organizing Committee appointed—presumably by the college president, upon the recommendation of the college librarian. The committee would work with the Librarian in determining what officers, executive council, and standing committees should be set up. Also consideration can be given to the need or desirability of a constitution and bylaws. Advice on all of these points, as well as a listing of Friends groups in the United States, can be secured by writing to the Library Administration Division of the American Library Association, 50 East Huron Street, Chicago, Illinois 60611.

When the Friends of the _____ College Library has been established, what continuing activities might it have? First of all, it is recommended that the members *give* something (annual dues, etc.) and they in return *receive* something. The first of the latter could well be a journal, modest initially but with good paper, format, and illustrations as soon as possible. Its main function would be to knit the group together by means of news about gifts to the Library and developments in the latter's staff, facilities, and services. At least one article about some important item in the library collection could be written by an appropriate subject specialist, but in a style that would be understandable to the reader who does not know the first thing about the subject. With the inclusion of human interest elements and an illustration or two, this concept can be extremely successful. (This has been the formula used to advantage in Columbia Library Columns, which is now beginning its twenty-first year of publication.) Three issues a year give the members a feeling that the association is active.

The same frequency is suggested for meetings of the Friends. These could simply be evening gatherings to hear a speaker; sociability can be furthered if they follow a modestly priced subscription dinner. An exhibit of recent important acquisitions would be of interest. As with the writers of articles indicated above, the speaker could well talk about some item or topic related to the Library's collections, but geared to an audience of laymen.

One additional point: When an active and enthusiastic Friends group has become operative, its members with their heightened personal interest in the Library will likewise feel a more direct interest in the college. As suggested above, this can be true whether the Friends' members are alumni of the college or not. In this period of economic pressures and problems, what could be more appealing to the college president than to have figuratively at his side this group which is so dedicated to developing the assets of the library and indirectly the welfare of the college as a whole?

It might be of interest to our readers here to know that the Friends of the Columbia Libraries, about the starting of which there was much discussion twenty years ago, have in the ensuing two decades given rarities and manuscripts appraised at $1,160,000 and, in addition, cash in excess of $340,000. The books and manuscripts were ones for the purchase of which no University funds would have been available. In the main they were items of distinction and value which will be the source for productive research on into the future. Meanwhile, they have come from private custody into institutional protection and have been prepared for research use.

Should the _____ College Library organize a Friends group? Consideration thereof is urged. The benefits to the Librarian, the Library, and the College could be substantial.[1]

Despite the upbeat tone of the above article, it should not be assumed automatically that every academic library should sponsor a Friends group. The cost in staff time could be enormous; the development of a collection of rarities and manuscripts in a working collection that does not now have such a collection and does not support research on the graduate level might be an expensive luxury. A library that does not have the appropriate physical conditions for the proper protection and preservation of rare books and manuscripts would be unwise to try to collect such material. It would be far wiser for such a library to specialize in areas of local concern—with or without a Friends of the Library group.

The Friends of the Library Committee of the Public Relations Section of the Library Administration Division of the American Library Association has issued the following statement:

What's a Friend for?

Just as a personal friend lends support, encouragement, interest and assistance, a Library Friend provides support to the staff and to the library image.

In a variety of ways, these volunteer groups are a multi-faceted public relations vehicle, providing services, money and encouragement to all types of libraries. The following activities are a sample of the incredibly diverse ways Friends act—as reported in a survey conducted by the Friends of the Library Committee:

SERVICES PROVIDED: clerical help, refreshments for programs, displays arranged, hospitals and shut-ins visited, equipment purchased, landscaping provided, general maintenance, etc.

MEMBERSHIP: provides information about libraries to non-users, can make library social focal point for the community.

PUBLIC RELATIONS: informs community of programs, activities, resources and needs of the library. Different programming can involve all strata of the community.

FUND-RAISING: book sales, author receptions, house tours, theatre parties, art shows, all are vehicles for making money.

ASSISTANCE: legislative advocacy, special projects, speaking at public meetings.

To learn who your closest Friends are, consult the 1978 Friends of Libraries Directory. Price of $6.50 postpaid from the publisher, the ALA Library Administration Division.

For the most current information about Friends' groups, consult *Friends of the Library—National Notebook,* a newsletter of the Friends of the Library Committee, Public Relations Section, Library Administration Division, ALA ($4.00 per year subscription). Also, the Library Administration Division collects Friends materials from Friends groups around the country. If your Friends group publishes brochures, leaflets, announcements or has bylaws or a newsletter, *send multiple copies* to the LAD Headquarters, 50 E. Huron Street, Chicago, IL 60611. Those materials are available free to those just starting a Friends group or to those looking for new ideas for activities and projects.[2]

TIPS ON SOLICITING GIFTS

An active policy on soliciting gifts means a constant awareness of what is or may be available. In the furtherance of this aim, many librarians have found it useful to become members of organizations such as the Junior Chamber of Commerce, the local chapter of the Lions Club, Kiwanis, or other such social groups. Being on friendly terms with local newspaper editors, all faculty members, heads of large law firms, and other businesses frequently may lead to acquiring funds for memorial gifts or the acquisition of collections built up over the years by retiring (or recently deceased) faculty members. Book review editors for newspapers and journals may be willing to contribute review copies or publications. Reading obituaries can also be a source of information about collections that could be obtained for the library if possible tax deductions are brought to the attention of the heirs. Finding other sources of information about gifts can be a real challenge to the librarian's ingenuity.

NOTES

1. Reprinted by permission of the American Library Association from "A Friends of the Library Group for My College?" by Charles W. Mixer, College Library Notes for the College President (Summer 1971), p. 1-4.

2. Letter statement to author from Sandy Dolnick, chairperson of the Friends of the Library, May 20, 1978.

ADDITIONAL REFERENCES

Briggs, Donald R. "Gift Appraisal Policy in Large Research Libraries." *College & Research Libraries* 29 (November 1968): 505-07.

Christian, R. "Gifts to Libraries: Advantages and Procedures." *Mississippi Library News* 35 (June 1971): 113-15.

Finch, H. "Gifts, Appraisals and Taxes." *Cornell University Library Bulletin,* no. 189 (May 1971): 7-10.

Gwyn, A., et al. "Friends of the Library." *College & Research Libraries* 36 (July 1975): 272-82. A 1974 survey covering origins, objectives, government of groups, revenues, activities, publications, and support.

Leab, K. K. and D. J. "Appraisal." In *Book Collecting: A Modern Guide,* edited by Jean Peters, pp. 183-96. New York: Bowker, 1977.

Society of American Archivists. College and University Archives Committee. "Forms manual." 1973. Section 2, on collecting policies and procedures, includes interesting examples of gift forms.

Szladits, L. L. "Arts and Craft of Collecting Manuscripts." In *Book Collecting: A Modern Guide,* edited by Jean Peters, pp. 74-96. New York: Bowker, 1977.

THE FRIENDS OF THE COLUMBIA LIBRARIES are a group whose members have welcomed an opportunity to associate themselves with the intellectual life of a great university through participating in a program centering on the Libraries of the Columbia Corporation. These Libraries circulate nearly 1,300,000 books a year, which is one of the highest circulation rates per academic user in the United States.

Privileges of Membership

• Invitations to exhibitions, lectures, and other special events. The Bancroft Awards Dinner is an important annual affair, and the Friends have entertained and been addressed by many distinguished persons in the academic and cultural world.

• Use of books in the reading rooms of the Libraries.

• Opportunity to consult Librarians, including those in charge of the specialized collections, about material of interest to a member. (Each Division Head has members' names on file.)

• Free subscription to COLUMBIA LIBRARY COLUMNS, an illustrated journal published by the Friends. It contains articles, both scholarly and in a lighter vein, relating to the world of books—and keeps its readers in touch with the most significant developments in the Libraries and their collections.

• Purchase of most Columbia University Press books at 20 per cent discount. (Please send requests for C. U. Press catalog and orders for books to the *Secretary-Treasurer of the Friends,* Columbia University, 535 West 114th Street, New York, New York 10027).

Membership

Classes of membership are indicated on the enclosed form. Part of each member's dues goes to support the Friends' program and the balance to the Friends' book account. Thus the larger the gift the more it will aid the Libraries' book resources.

Helping the Libraries to Grow

THE FRIENDS HAVE ASSISTED THE COLUMBIA Libraries in several direct ways: first, through their active interest in the institution and its ideals and through promoting public interest in the role of a research library in education; second, through gifts of books, manuscripts and other useful materials; and third, through financial contributions.

Of special interest to our members is the establishment by the Council of the Friends of an "Endowment Fund," inaugurated a few years ago with a nucleus of $25,000. The earnings from the fund are to be used for the purchase of rare books and manuscripts in all fields. We hope that the fund will grow to become a major resource. Members who wish a part of their regular contribution to be added to the endowment fund may stipulate this in their response to our annual appeal.

By helping preserve the intellectual accomplishment of the past, we lay the foundation for the university of the future. This is the primary purpose of the Friends of the Columbia Libraries.

Statement by a typical Friends of Library group. Reprinted by permission of the Friends of Columbia Libraries.

5 | Selection and Dispersal of Gifts and Exchanges

It should be recognized that items received as either gifts or exchanges are fully as important as purchased materials and as such deserve the same degree of care and expedience in processing. There is a psychological tendency in many libraries to overlook this fact, especially when large collections are involved, with the result that backlogs of unprocessed and even unreviewed titles develop. This means not only that the books or serials are not available to the library clientele but also that costly storage problems may evolve.

Ideally, as gifts are received, recorded, and acknowledged, they are culled to remove materials not worthy of further consideration: items in poor physical condition, trade paperback books, reprints of articles (usually), non-library materials, obviously outdated texts, materials out of the collecting scope of the library, and so forth. But items of primary use presumably already in one library's collection may well be secondarily useful in another. This would be true of a reference book that is updated every year or two. The most recently superseded volume could be useful in a library that does not consider it of such primary importance that budgeted funds should be used for its purchase, especially if the item is expensive. Examples of this type of material would be *The World of Learning* and *Books in Print*.

If it is known in advance that the gift or exchange item is wanted for a particular use in the library, processing to assimilate it into the collection should begin immediately. This would be true, of course, when the item has been solicited.

For the rest of the materials, some method should be instituted to bring the titles to the attention of appropriate selection officers. Usually this is done by providing an area of shelving where materials can be displayed for review on a regular basis. If books are arranged in rough subject categories, the selection process is made easier.

Identification of the source of each item is important. This can be done by inserting inside the front cover of each book a scrap card or slip containing the most basic information, such as "Gift of Mary C. Public," or "In memory of Donald Z. Presto." These can be typed, handwritten, rubber stamped, or made from an Addressograph plate or similar mechanical means. This process may not be necessary if all materials in any selection group are from the same source. There is no point in marking the books themselves until it is decided which books are needed or wanted.

A simple selection form can then be used by those reviewing the titles to indicate the disposition to be made. The sample form below can be adapted for use in a local situation.

SELECTION SLIP FOR GIFT AND EXCHANGE MATERIALS

1. Wanted for _____ only if new to this Dept.
   (location)

2. Wanted for _____ even as added copy.
   (location)

3. Wanted for _____ only if new to (institution).
   (location)

4. Wanted for _____ uncataloged.
   (location)

5. Wanted for further examination in _____.
   (location)

6. Not wanted in _____, but offer to _____.
   (location)   (location)

Such a form can be useful to library staff, faculty members, students, or other interested parties, subject to review, of course, by the appropriate personnel.

Once the examination period is over and all selection personnel have reviewed the books, the group can be removed and replaced by a new group. Books with no selection slips can be set aside for other uses (see chapter 6). Any book with more than one selection slip may require setting priorities or making judgments. For example, if two or more libraries (or branches, departments, or units) have indicated on line 1 of the form that they wish this title, priorities should be assigned so that if the library with the highest priority already has this title, it can then be searched for the library with the next priority. If this kind of conflict arises through marking line 2, or a combination of lines 1 and 2, a judgment will have to be made.

When making such judgments, what factors should be considered? Appropriateness is one of the most important. To what extent does the item fit within the collecting policy of one library (or branch) as opposed to another? Relatively how important is the item to one library as opposed to another? Obviously, if one library needs the book because it has been placed on reserve (showing a presumed immediate demand), this library should be favored over another desiring the book only for adjunct purposes. If one library wished the book "even as added copy" while a second wants the book only if it is not presently part of its collection, thought should be given to "spreading the wealth." The selector who marked "even as added copy" probably has in mind that there is already one copy in his collection. Perhaps, then, it would be wiser to place the book in the library that presumably does not have a copy, the better to build up and round out its collection—if it is truly appropriate.

Line 4 would be used for items to be used internally, for example, office reference, or for vertical files, and so on. Line 5 would be marked for checking edition, condition, need for reserve, and the like. Line 6 would be used for a book that crosses collection scope lines; a book on business law might be housed in a business library or in a law library. This line would also be used to recommend for use outside the library system, perhaps to offer it to an affiliated institution or to USBE.

Only the books selected for inclusion in the library's collections would be permanently marked for source and ownership. Marking books that are not going to be retained only reduces their resale value. Only the items selected would be searched in files, catalogs, lists, or other bibliographic records. It would be a waste of time and money to search everything.

6 | Disposition of Unwanted Materials

Every library, from time to time, has materials it neither needs nor wants.[1] The problem of how best to dispose of these can sometimes be troublesome. Many libraries consider the disposal process as concomitant to the acquisition process. Hence, organizationally, disposal activities fall within the technical services area, and the gift and exchange unit seems a logical agency to oversee the process.

Materials for disposal can come from a variety of sources: from the weeding process, which produces duplicate copies, worn or mutilated copies, superseded titles, and disfigured books; duplicate copies received as gifts; gifts that do not fit within collecting policies; purchases that are inadvertant duplicates and non-returnable. In a large library system the volume of such materials can be staggering.

THROWING AWAY

There are four basic ways to get rid of unwanted library materials: they can be thrown away, given away, exchanged, or sold. It would seem fairly obvious that such disposal should be made to the library's best advantage, and first priority should be given to reuse within the library system or parent organization. An item discarded by one unit may well be useful in another. Assuming that all such uses have been considered, the next step is to discard all materials that, for whatever reason, would have little or no potential value to someone else. These would include volumes worn or mutilated beyond repair, books whose content is completely outdated (watching, however, for items that might be of interest to a collector), and items whose paper is too brittle to be useful. Before actually discarding (or otherwise disposing of) materials bearing library ownership marks, such ownership should be negated by stamping with some term like "withdrawn," "sold," or "canceled." Doing so will obviate the chance that someone will return the book to the library thinking he has done his good deed for the day. Such cancellation marks should appear only on the book plate or other ownership designation to prevent unnecessary defacement.

Throwing away books sounds like a simple procedure; you just put them into a waste basket, and the maintenance people somehow make them disappear. But this is not so when there is a large quantity of books to be destroyed. One or two books at a time will probably present no problem, but the weeding process could produce two or three hundred volumes which seem to have no potential use. If they are put with the regular trash, someone will inevitably paw through them and raise a great hue and cry about the library's throwing away valuable books. When Columbia University tried to discard old and flaking volumes of newspapers which it had replaced with microfilm copies, there ensued a brouhaha that reached national proportions (*Library Journal,* January 1, 1972, p. 23).

The Massachusetts Division of Library Extension issued some very good advice to its constituents when it wrote,

In all cases, dispose of books quietly. Do not give publicity to the process. The librarian, with the consent of the trustees, should attend to this disposal rather than depend upon an unreliable person; otherwise, the books may turn up in the library at a later date. There will be many townspeople who will not try to understand the need for discarding; they will be the first at town meetings to advocate a cut in the library budget, reasoning that the library has so much money, its librarian is throwing books away in an effort to expend it.[2]

Waste paper dealers will not handle discarded books unless they are stripped of their covers—a costly process. Most libraries do not have access to an incinerator. If there is a commercial shredder that can handle books, its cost must be prohibitive, and the knowledge of its possession or use by the library would be very poor public relations. The only other choice would seem to be commercial or public waste disposal. The New York Public Library solves the problem by using a dumpster in which nothing may be thrown except paper products. Each time the dumpster is filled, a commercial firm hauls it away and replaces it with an empty dumpster. This is fine if there is a suitable place to house the dumpster where it is not accessible to the public. Monetary returns are small, but the fact of removal of unwanted books is its own reward. This is especially fortunate in a situation in which the library is prohibited from selling materials bought with city or state funds. Many libraries are enjoined from selling materials that, in the larger sense, belong to their governing body (state, county, municipality, and so on). The same might apply to giving away materials. True, any department of the city or any recognized nonprofit organization may avail itself of the unwanted books before destruction.

Kemp mentions a special kind of caveat in discarding manuscripts.

Because of the personal nature of manuscript discards, some care should be given to what goes into the trash, where papers, bills, and cancelled checks are available for inspection. Many stamp or cover collectors, amateur bookmen, and book scouts enjoy prowling; the librarian would not want someone to ask the donor about further envelopes or magazines, mentioning all those items he had found in the library's trash. There is already much negative publicity about school librarians burning or destroying books; pulping unwanted books and manuscripts is a necessity, but it should be done with discretion.[3]

GIVING AWAY

Every large library frequently receives appeals from other libraries less fortunate and from social interest groups, such as prisons, drug rehabilitation groups, and inner-city welfare groups. Gifts judiciously made to such organizations can rebound favorably to the library in publicity and community service. Again, costs must be considered. Is the library willing to devote personnel time to selection, packing, and shipping? It might be more effective to ask a representative of the organization to select, pack, and remove the materials.

Sometimes books and journals can be handled effectively through the "largesse" offers in the newsletters of library organizations. However, this may mean storing the materials for a period of time that may be unacceptable—time for the newsletter to be issued, mailed, read, and acted upon.

EXCHANGE

Offering unwanted materials to exchange partners is a way of putting books to good use, but the cost of listing, as discussed in chapter 3, can be considerable. Again, if a representative of the exchange partner will select and remove from the shelves directly, the cost will be much less. However, the quality of materials available may well be worth the cost of listing, especially if other exchange materials are scarce. Listings on sheets are less costly than listings on individual slips, not only in time consumed and supplies but in postage paid. The major advantage of individual listings on slips is their flexibility. Slips can be rearranged as the occasion demands, removed when materials are no longer available, and annotated on the reverse to show which exchange partners have already examined them.

SELLING

Books and periodicals available for disposal can be sold in a variety of ways and may add substantially to the library's coffers. They can be sold to dealers, to other libraries, to the library's constituency, to the general public, or through auction.

Selling to dealers can be very fruitful. Some libraries do this on a regular basis, periodically making materials available for selection or for accepting bids for the lot (or lots). In the case of selection, the librarian should review the materials and either ask what the dealer will pay or set an asking price for the library. Here it is important to keep in mind that the dealer must add on his costs as well as a profit margin and still be able to sell at a fair price. A possible way of approaching this is to imagine the resale price and then figure that one-third of that price represents the cost to the dealer when he buys the books, one-third is his overhead in preparing the books for resale, and one-third represents his profit. This, of course, is only a generalization, but it will set the frame of mind when determining how much the library should receive. It is understood that the costs of packing and removing the materials will be borne by the buyer, whether he carries them out to his own car or asks that they be shipped.

Many libraries are not located geographically or strategically to make periodic sales to dealers feasible. In this case, some libraries make arrangements with a dealer who will agree to handle all the materials that a library has for disposition. In arrangements of this sort, however, the amount received by the library will be less than if the dealer bought selectively.

When selling books or journals directly to another library the approach is somewhat different. Since there is no middleman and profit does not have to be considered, the selling library can expect to receive somewhat more than a dealer would be willing to pay, but still less than what the buying library would pay in the open market.

Selling to the library's constituency is advantageous from the standpoint of incoming funds as well as from the good will it engenders. Again, the question of space arises: where to hold the book sale? Should it be on a continuing basis or periodically? Some libraries have an annual or a semiannual book fair in an unused classroom, a nearby parking lot, a tent, a hallway, or wherever else ingenuity can devise. Pricing can pose a problem in terms of knowing values and using personnel time to mark the books individually. Setting a flat price per volume can obviate these difficulties. The price should include sales tax, if applicable.

Since the library is presumably not in competition with the local commercial market but is serving its own needs by disposing of unwanted materials and also serving its clientele by providing materials at low prices, the flat price (or any price) set should be determined, at least to some degree, by considering the cost of handling and storing.

The question will naturally arise as to what is salable. The answer, oddly enough, is almost anything that is still in usable condition. The problem is finding the right market. A 1913 volume on agricultural statistics in India will probably not interest 99 percent of the buying public, but it may be just the right thing for a person who is writing a dissertation on the agricultural history of India in the twentieth century. Similarly, railroad timetables from Eastern Europe will not be on the best-seller list but may give a great deal of pleasure to a railroad buff.

Selling journals (odd issues or runs) entails its own set of problems. Ordinarily there is little market for these among the library's clientele, although there are exceptions. The student of international affairs may well be interested in back issues of *Foreign Affairs,* or the collector may be interested in filling in his set of *Horizon.* More likely, journals will find another home in the Universal Serials and Book Exchange (USBE) or with dealers who specialize in back issues. However, certain journals seem to have little or no afterlife. Weekly news magazines like *Newsweek, Time,* and *U.S. News and World Report* do not have much market value; nor do esoteric journals with small circulations. Other journals are in such wide circulation, like the *Journal of the American Medical Association,* or have only local and timely appeal *(Cue, TV Guide, New York Magazine),* and should be discarded immediately. Then again, dealers' supplies vary from time to time, and what is not needed now may be in some demand three months from now. Generally speaking, the USBE can use many titles that commercial dealers do not find it practical to stock.

It has been implied up to this point that monies received from the sale of library materials will come to the library. This is not always the case; the parent institution may claim such proceeds as part of its general income. The argument can be made, however, that such income would help to make the gift and exchange unit become self-supporting—at least to the extent of providing the funds used for buying materials to be sent on exchange. The income from the book sale to faculty and students would certainly pay the salaries or wages of those who run the sale. In some cases such income is used to defray the overdraft of budgeted book accounts.

INVOICING

Invoicing sales, be they duplicate books and journals, publications of the library, or services rendered (for example, prepaid postage that must be refunded), is an item which should not be overlooked and which should be provided for in advance. A simple invoice form should contain certain basic elements: the exact name and address of the billing institution, the name and address of the person or organization being billed, date of the invoice, invoice number, a description of the material sold, the price per unit and the total amount, terms of sale, indication of to whom the check should be written, a space for the buyer's purchase order number or other reference, and possibly the account number to which the money should be credited when received. Sample invoices appear in Appendix E.

AUCTIONS

Auction sales are useful in disposing of valuable items, but auction houses will not usually handle items worth less than fifteen dollars each (although lesser-value items can be batched). Single titles or groups of materials are suitable for auction if their value is great enough. The commission paid to the auction house is usually 20-25 percent, with a minimum of ten dollars. Payment for items sold at auction is usually made six weeks after the date of sale.

In addition to negating marks of ownership before disposing of materials, another precaution should be taken: remove all loose papers or other materials that might be in the books. The purpose for this procedure is twofold: to prevent any possible embarrassment to previous owners and to discover and capture any papers of value. Quite often important autograph letters or other manuscripts are stuck in books. It is amazing to see the numbers and kinds of things that previous owners had used as book marks or left in books quite unintentionally. This includes money, post cards (these can be given or sold to collectors), envelopes with foreign (or domestic) stamps, mementos of various kinds, newspaper clippings (which if left in books tend to discolor the pages), pencils, paper clips, rubber bands— the list is endless. The discovery of such items tends to relieve the tedium of the routine of riffling through the pages of each book before it leaves the library's possession.

Games, ties, souvenirs, coins, pictures, statuary, and other such items often appear in gifts—they might be called "gifts within gifts"—and can be offered to the local rummage sale, provided there is no possibility of embarrassing the donor.

NOTES

1. Portions of this chapter originally were published in Alfred H. Lane, "Options for Book Disposal," *The De-Acquisitions Librarian* 1, no. 2 (Summer 1976): 7-8.

2. Massachusetts Division of Library Extension, "Weeding the Library: Selection in Reverse" (Based on material prepared by the Public Library Supervisors, Division of Library Extension, University of the State of New York and adapted for Massachusetts by the Massachusetts Division of Library Extension, 6th rev. ed., October 1963).

3. Edward C. Kemp, *Manuscript Solicitation for Libraries, Special Collections, Museums, and Archives* (Littleton, Colo.: Libraries Unlimited, 1978), p. 66.

ADDITIONAL REFERENCE

Wolf, Edwin, II. "Fine Art of Selling Duplicates." *Antiquarian Bookman's Yearbook* (1968): 3-5. A cogent and witty essay on the sale of books by auction and sale to dealers.

7 | Rare Books and Manuscripts

Most libraries with special collections of rare books and manuscripts rely primarily on gifts for building up these collections. It is a rare library, indeed, that can afford many purchases in this area. A decision by the Internal Revenue Service a few years ago to the effect that gifts of creativity, such as manuscripts, are not tax deductible changed the giving pattern by authors to some extent. However, a way around this has proved helpful to libraries. A third party (a relative, friend, another institution, and so on) may deduct the full market value of the gift.

One basic precept to be observed is to collect rare books or manuscripts only in areas where they will support research within the scope of the library's collecting policies. In other words, do not accept what you cannot use—or foresee a use for. Prospective donors who offer gifts that are out of this scope should be referred to another institution.

In developing a collection of rare books and manuscripts it is easiest and best to build on strength. A collection of materials on local history, for example, is likely to attract more of the same, and each addition not only strengthens the total collection but, with appropriate publicity, will draw other such gifts. Diaries, genealogical records, oral history interviews, and other reminiscences tend to mesh with each other, especially when paths of individual careers have touched or crossed.

This thought leads to another very important consideration: personal privacy. In accepting manuscript materials there are legal considerations to be met. It should be made clear who owns the literary rights to the papers. Personal privacy should be a prime concern, especially in terms of diaries or correspondence concerning living persons or those who have died but recently. Manuscript material by its very nature is unique, and controls must be maintained to guard against personal loss or embarrassment. In this matter, however, any restrictions made by the donor on the use of the material should be pared down to the lowest acceptable minimum, made more palatable, perhaps, if given the option to renew when the time limit has expired.

Concerning a recent gift of correspondence files to a medical library, the highly respected dealer who was asked to appraise the collection cautioned the donor as follows:

> As a librarian and student of history I should say that I abhor any restriction being made on a gift of this kind. You may not, however, have looked at some of the family files . . . for some time though, so you may not recollect their highly personal nature. I feel that if it matters you might want to consider a ten or twenty-five year seal on the personal family papers. My recommendation is not to do anything like this because I cannot see anything in the files that would be harmful to reasonable people; nevertheless, some indiscretions of the family are there and I do not want to ignore the idea of a seal carelessly.

There can be no restrictions on the use of books except in terms of actual ownership or physical handling for protection. Additionally, there can be no library-imposed restrictions on use (except physical handling) in a tax-free institution.

A major key in the development of special collections of this kind is publicity, not only as a means of indicating availability but also to encourage others to give similar materials. Press releases, exhibits, activities of Friends groups, and notices to faculty and other scholars are all appropriate means to these ends.

There are several excellent books and articles on the various aspects of soliciting, caring for, and controlling rare books and manuscripts, and it is not within the scope of this volume to go into the details of this very specialized area. However, a few basic words should be mentioned about care and preservation. Initially, it should be pointed out that to accept a gift of rare or manuscript items without the means to care for them properly would be a disservice to the scholarly world. Proper atmospheric control—temperature, humidity, cleanliness—as well as proper physical housing—acid-free containers, adequate space, freedom from possibly damaging materials—are essential considerations which must be secured before acceptance of such a gift can be considered. The use of these rarities must also be controlled. The use, or even presence, of a fountain pen, for instance, should be absolutely forbidden to those studying manuscripts.

ADDITIONAL REFERENCES

Duckett, Kenneth W. *Modern Manuscripts: A Practical Manual for Their Management, Care, and Use.* Nashville, Tenn.: American Association for

State and Local History, 1975. See chapter 3 on the mechanics and ethics of acquisitions and the directory of appraisers. This is a history of manuscript collecting, administration, acquisition, care, use, and so forth. It contains a directory of associations, publications, equipment, supplies and services, glossary, and bibliography.

Guidelines on Manuscripts and Archives Adopted by the Association of College and Research Libraries. Chicago: ACRL, 1977. This includes statements on the appraisal of gifts and on legal title, and a universal gift form and instructions.

Kemp, Edward C. *Manuscript Solicitation for Libraries, Special Collections, Museums, and Archives.* Littleton, Colo.: Libraries Unlimited, 1978.

IRS Deduction Guidelines

INTRODUCTION

Our Federal Government recognized that gifts to religious, educational, charitable, scientific, and literary organizations have contributed significantly to the welfare of our nation; and the tax laws are designed to encourage such giving. You are entitled to take a charitable contribution deduction, subject to certain conditions and limitations, on your income tax return for genuine gifts of cash or property to such qualified organizations. In the case of property other than cash, the amount of the deduction is the fair market value of the property, reduced in some cases by all or part of any appreciation in value. In all cases, the fair market value is the starting point for determining your allowable contribution deduction.

How do you determine the fair market value of donated noncash property? This is a difficult question to answer with respect to many types of property. Unfortunately, you can rarely evaluate property by using fixed rules or formulas, or other simple solutions. Often, the valuation of property will require you, or appraisers, to consider and to weigh numerous factors.

The purpose of this publication is to provide assistance to individuals, appraisers, and valuation groups in evaluating the noncash property donated to qualified organizations. It also sets forth the information you may be required to supply to the Internal Revenue Service to support the deduction you claim on your income tax return. The rules relating to charitable contributions other than those rules concerning the determination and support of fair market value are not discussed in this publication. A comprehensive discussion of these other rules can be found in Publication 526, *Income Tax Deduction for Contributions,* which may be obtained free from your nearest Internal Revenue office.

---

*Excerpted from U.S., Department of the Treasury, Internal Revenue Service, *Valuation of Donated Property,* Publication no. 451, 1978.

FAIR MARKET VALUE

Fair market value is defined as the price at which the property would change hands between a willing buyer and a willing seller, neither being under any compulsion to buy or sell and both having reasonable knowledge of the relevant facts.

Since it does not ordinarily lend itself to fixed rules or formulas, fair market value is determined by considering all the factors that reasonably bear on determining the price that would be agreed upon between the willing buyer and the willing seller who are not under any compulsion to act and who have reasonable knowledge of the facts. . . .

MAKING THE VALUATION OF PROPERTY

In making (and proving) the valuation of property you donate to a charitable organization, you must consider all factors bearing on its value that are relevant and include, when applicable, the cost or selling price of the item, sales of comparable property, cost of replacement, opinion evidence, valuation date, and appraisals.

COST OR SELLING PRICE

The best evidence of the fair market value of donated property may be the property's cost or actual selling price within a reasonable time before or after the valuation date. This is assuming that such purchase or sale was at arm's length and that both parties were fully informed as to all relevant facts.

If the purchase or sale was not within reasonable proximity to the date of the contribution (valuation date), little weight can be given to evidence of your cost or the selling price. Conditions are always changing; consequently, the value of the selling price as a factor in the valuation process lessens upon the widening of the time interval. . . .

A bona fide offer to purchase near the valuation date may help to prove the value of the donated property if the prospective purchaser was willing to complete the transaction and was able to carry it out. To rely on an offer, you should be able to show evidence of the offer and the specific amount to be paid under it. Offers to purchase property other than the donated item will not serve as proof of value unless there is reasonable similarity in quality and value to the donated property. . . .

COST OF REPLACEMENT

The cost of acquiring, constructing, or manufacturing property similar to the donated item may be considered in determining fair market value if it can be shown that there is a reasonable relationship between cost of replacement and fair market value. The cost of replacement is the amount it would cost to replace the donated item on the valuation date. Frequently, no relationship exists between the cost of replacement and fair market value. The supply of the donated property may be more or less than the demand for the property—thus reducing the value of the replacement cost as a factor to consider. . . .

GIFTS OF APPRECIATED PROPERTY

If you donate property with a fair market value that is greater than your basis in the property, you may have to reduce the fair market value by all or a portion of the appreciation when computing your deduction. The amount of the reduction depends on whether the property is ordinary income property or capital gain property.

Ordinary income property is property that, if sold, would result in ordinary income or short-term capital gain. Examples of ordinary income property are inventory, a copyright, a literary, musical or artistic composition given by the creating artist, letters and memorandums given by the person who prepared them (or the person for whom they were prepared), and capital stock held 9 months or less in 1977 (one year or less in 1978 and later years).

The deduction for a gift of ordinary income property is limited to the fair market value less the amount that would be ordinary income. . . .

LETTERS AND MEMORANDUMS

Any letters, memorandums, or similar property donated by the person who created them or the person for whom they were created, are considered ordinary income property, and the deduction is limited to the fair market value reduced by the amount of appreciation over cost or other adjusted basis.

Similar property includes, for example, such property as a draft of a speech, a manuscript, a research paper, an oral recording of any type, a transcript of an oral recording, a transcript of an oral interview or of dictation, a personal diary, a business diary, a log or a journal, a corporate archive, including a corporate charter, office correspondence, a financial record, a drawing, a photograph, or a dispatch.

A letter, memorandum, or similar property addressed to a taxpayer shall be considered as prepared or produced for the taxpayer. These rules do not apply to property such as corporate archives, records, or correspondence sold or disposed of as part of a going business if such property has no significant value separate and apart from its relation to, and use in, such business.

Generally, property is created in whole or in part by the personal efforts of a taxpayer if such taxpayer performs literary, theatrical, musical, artistic, or other creative or productive work which affirmatively contributes to the creation of the property, or if such taxpayer directs and guides others in the performance of such work.

A letter, memorandum, or similar property which is prepared by personnel who are under the administrative control of a taxpayer, such as a corporate executive, is considered to have been prepared or produced by the executive whether or not the material is reviewed by that person.

GOVERNMENT PUBLICATIONS

After October 4, 1976, U.S. Government publications (including the Congressional Record) which you receive from the Government without charge or below the price at which they are sold to the general public are considered ordinary income property. If you later contribute these publications to a charity, the value of your contribution is limited to the amount, if any, which you paid for the publications.

If you acquire any Government publications from another individual who received them without charge or below the price at which they are sold to the general public, your basis in such publications, for tax purposes, is the same as that of the individual who originally received them. . . .

PROBLEMS IN DETERMINING FAIR MARKET VALUE

There are a number of pitfalls to be avoided in evaluating donated noncash property. A few of the more common ones follow.

The valuation of donated property would be a simple matter if you could rely solely on fixed formulas, rules, or methods. Unfortunately, usually it is not that simple; moreover, using such formulas, etc., will seldom result in an acceptable determination of fair market value. There is no single formula, rule, or method that is universally applicable to determine the value of an item of property. This is not to say that a valuation may rest on mere speculation—to the contrary, you must consider all the facts and circumstances connected with the property. For example, it is erroneous to evaluate donated furniture at the fixed rate of 15% of replacement cost. The furniture, at the date of contribution, may be out-of-style of in poor condition—thus having little if any value. On the other hand, it may include antiques, the value of which could not easily be determined by using such a formula.

FAIR MARKET PRICE

In the absence of exceptional circumstances, the sale price of property in arm's length transactions in an open market is the best evidence of its value. When sales of comparable property are relied on, the sales must have been made in an open market. . . .

Example. You donate a rare old book to your former college. The book is a second edition in poor condition because of a missing back cover. You ascertain that there was a sale, near the valuation date, of the first edition of the book in good condition. Although the contents are the same, the dissimilarity (different editions and conditions) between the two books is so great that the sale price of the comparative is virtually useless for valuation purposes. . . .

APPRAISALS

You may find it necessary to hire one or more experts to gather and analyze all the facts in their appraisals of your donated property. When it becomes necessary to get an appraisal to determine the value of your charitable contribution, a signed copy of the appraisal report should accompany your income tax return. The more complete the information filed with a tax return, the more unlikely it will be that the Internal Revenue Service will find it necessary to question items on it. Thus, when reporting a deduction for charitable contributions, you will facilitate the review and the acceptance of the amounts reported if you attach to your return copies of any appraisals that you have secured.

The weight given an appraisal depends upon the appraiser and the completeness of the appraisal report. A satisfactory appraisal discusses all the facts on which an intelligent judgment of valuation should be based. Many of the facts that must be considered are discussed in this publication. The appraisal may not be given any weight if:

(1)   All the applicable factors are not considered;
(2)   Little more than a statement of opinion is given;
(3)   The opinion is not consistent with known factors;
(4)   The opinion is beyond reason and is arbitrary.

Appraisals should be made at a date as close to the valuation date as possible. An appraisal that is not made within reasonable proximity to the valuation date may be afforded less weight, as the appraiser may be considered to be less knowledgeable of market conditions on the valuation date.

Appraisals are not always necessary. This is particularly true for minor items of property, or when you can easily determine the value of property by other methods.

THE APPRAISER

The weight given an appraisal depends upon, in addition to the completeness of the report, the appraiser's familiarity with the property, experience, background, and knowledge of the facts at the time of the contribution. However, despite the qualifications, an appraiser's opinion will not be given weight if it is clearly opposed to common sense and the existent facts. The appraiser's opinion is never more important than the facts upon which it is based.

Membership in appraisal organizations will not automatically establish the appraiser's competency. Nor will the absence of certificates, memberships, and the like automatically detract from the competency that otherwise exists.

Sometimes, an appraisal will be given less weight if the appraiser is associated with either the donor or the charitable organization. While not the situation in most cases, appraisers who are associated—other than for making the instant appraisal—with either of the parties to the contribution have rendered appraisals that were essentially nothing more than shams devised to give the color of legitimacy to grossly inflated valuation figures. The opinion of an expert is not binding on the Internal Revenue Service; moreover, all the facts associated with the donation may be considered.

COST OF APPRAISALS

Fees paid for appraisals of your donated property are not deductible as a charitable contribution. However, if the appraisals were made to determine the amounts to be entered as a charitable contribution on your income tax return, the fees would qualify as a miscellaneous deduction in Schedule A (Form 1040).

APPRAISAL FORMAT

In general, an appraisal report should contain at least the following:

(1) A summary of the appraiser's qualifications to appraise this particular property;
(2) A statement of the value and the appraiser's definition of how that value was obtained;
(3) A full and complete description of the article to be valued;
(4) The bases upon which the appraisal was made, including any restrictions, understandings, or covenants limiting the use or disposition of the property;
(5) The date the property was valued;
(6) The signature of the appraiser and the date the appraisal was made. . . .

COLLECTIONS

There are many types of collections that may be the subject of a charitable donation—so many that it would not be practical to discuss them all in this publication. Most popular are: rare books, autographs, manuscripts, stamps, coins, guns, phonograph records, dolls, and natural history items. Many of the elements of valuation that apply to paintings and other objects of art, discussed earlier, also apply to miscellaneous collections.

REFERENCE MATERIAL

Publications available to assist you in the valuation of many types of collections include catalogs, dealers' price lists, bibliographies, text books, and other materials that help in determining fair market value. However, not all of these sources are always reliable indicators of fair market value.

For example, a dealer may sell an item for considerably less than shown on a price list after the item has remained unsold for a long period of time. Or the price that an item sold for in an auction may have been the result of a rigged sale. The expert appraiser generally can analyze the reference material and recognize and make adjustments for misleading entries. Therefore, if you are donating a valuable collection, you should secure one or more expert appraisals. If your donation appears to be of small value, you may be able to make a satisfactory valuation using reference materials available at a local public library. If your local library does not have the necessary material, your librarian can often order it from the city or state library systems.

BOOKS, MANUSCRIPTS, AUTOGRAPHS AND RELATED ITEMS

The principal method for determining the value of books, manuscripts, autographs, and related items is by selecting comparable sales and adjusting such price according to the differences between the comparatives and the item being evaluated. This is a complex and technical task that, except for a collection of small value, should be left to the expert appraiser. Dealers frequently specialize in certain areas such as Americana, foreign imports, Bibles, and scientific books, and have the experience and knowledge to evaluate collections in their specialties.

If the collection you are donating is of modest value, not requiring a formal written appraisal, the following information may assist you in determining fair market value.

BOOKS

The fact that a book is very old, or even very rare, does not necessarily mean that it is valuable. There are many books that are extremely old or rare, and that have little or no value. The serious collector is willing to pay good money for important books—books that are of great literary, scientific, historical, or other significance, and are in short supply.

The condition of the book has a great deal of influence on its value. Collectors are interested in items that are in fine, or at least good condition. When a book has a missing page, a loose binding, tears, stains, or is otherwise in poor condition, its value is greatly diminished.

Some other important factors in the valuation of a book are the type of binding (fine contemporary leather, cloth, paper), page (plain or gilt edged), and illustrations (drawings, photographs, colored or plain). Collectors usually seek out first editions of books; however, because of changes or additions, other editions are sometimes worth as much as, or more than, the first edition. Reference material helpful in the valuation of books can be found in, or obtained through, your local public library.

Some reference material that can assist you in evaluating books and pamphlets includes the following:

Bradley, Van Allen. *The New Gold in Your Attic.* New York, 1968. This reference and *The Book Collector's Handbook of Values,* 1972 and the revised edition, 1975, G. P. Putnam's Sons, contain helpful hints in evaluating your books and pamphlets; also price indexes based on auction and dealers' catalog prices.

Heard, J. Norman. *Bookman's Guide to Americana.* Scarecrow Press, 1971. The third edition was published in 1964, 4th edition in 1967, 5th edition in 1969, and 6th edition in 1971. Editions contain compilations of book prices taken from out-of-print booksellers' catalogs.

Leab, Katherine K. and Daniel J., eds., *American Book Prices Current.* New York, 1970-75. This guide contains a record of the prices paid for literary properties at auction sales in the United States and London. It lists those items that sold for $20 or more and is published annually, with 5-year cumulations.

Mandeville, Mildred S. *The Used Book Price Guide.* Price Guide Publishers, Kenmore, Washington, 1973. Part 1 was updated in 1966, Part 2 in 1963, Part 3 in 1964, and the new 5-year edition in 1972-1973. The text serves as an aid in ascertaining current prices.

McGrath, Daniel. *Bookman's Price Index.* Detroit, Michigan, 1972-1973. An annual guide to the values of rare and other out-of-print books and sets of periodicals.

Other useful reference material may be available at or through your local public library.

There are currently useful price guides in specialized fields, such as Civil War books, cookbooks, and Horatio Alger books. These may be available in the local public library, along with bibliographies, checklists, etc., useful in identifying first editions or other significant editions.

Manuscripts, autographs, diaries, and related items, that are handwritten, or at least signed by, the famous and the infamous, often are in demand and valuable. The writings of unknowns also may be of value if they are of historical, literary, or other importance. The valuation of such material is difficult. For example, there may be a considerable difference in value between two diaries that were kept by a famous person—one kept during boyhood and the other during an important period in the person's career. The expert appraiser can determine a value in these cases by applying knowledge and judgment to factors such as comparable sales and dealers' prices. The condition of the item is always important.

Signatures, or sets of signatures, that were cut off letters or other papers, usually have little or no value. However, complete sets of the signatures of the U.S. Presidents are in demand. . . .

INTRODUCTION*

You may deduct charitable contributions of money or property made to certain qualified organizations if you itemize your deductions on Scheule A (Form 1040). Generally, you may deduct up to 50% of your adjusted gross income, but 20% and 30% limitations apply in some cases.

*Excerpted from U.S., Department of the Treasury, Internal Revenue Service, *Income Tax Deduction for Contributions,* Publication no. 526, 1978.

Contributions must be paid in cash or other property before the close of your tax year to be deductible. This applies whether you use the cash or accrual method. Thus, you may deduct contributions charged to a bank credit card only in the year you actually pay the bank.

TIME OF CONTRIBUTION

Ordinarily, a contribution is considered made at the time of its unconditional delivery. For example, a check that you mail to a charity that later clears the bank is considered delivered on the date of mailing. The gift to a charity of a properly endorsed stock certificate is completed on the date of mailing or other delivery.

On the other hand, if you deliver a stock certificate for transfer into the name of the charity, your gift is not completed until the date the stock is transferred on the books of the issuing corporation.

Issuance and delivery of a promissory note to a charitable organization does not give rise to a deduction. However, a deduction is allowable when the note payments are actually made.

QUALIFIED ORGANIZATIONS

A contribution is deductible if it is made to, or for the use of, any of the following organizations:

A community chest, corporation, trust, fund, or foundation organized or created in the United States or its possessions, or under the laws of the United States, any state, the District of Columbia, or any possession of the United States, and organized and operated exclusively for charitable, religious, educational, scientific or literary purposes, or for the prevention of cruelty to children or animals, or to foster national or international amateur sports competition (but only if no part of its activities involves the provision of athletic facilities or equipment).

Examples of these types of organizations include:

Churches, synagogues, or other religious organizations;

Most educational organizations;

Recognized charitable nonprofit hospitals and medical research organizations. . . .

WHAT IS DEDUCTIBLE

Generally you may deduct your contributions of money or property made to qualified organizations. However, some contributions of service or contributions that result in personal benefit may not be deductible. . . .

BENEFITS RECEIVED BY DONORS

A contribution is deductible only if the value of the contribution exceeds any consideration or benefit to the donor. For example, if you buy bonds issued by a church to finance a new building, the purchase price of the bonds is not deductible as a contribution. If you later donate the bonds to the church, however, you then become entitled to a deduction. See *Gifts of Property.* . . .

GIFTS OF PROPERTY

If you donate property other than money to a qualified organization, you may generally deduct the fair market value of the property at the time of the contribution. However, if the property has appreciated in value, some adjustments may have to be made. See *Gifts of Appreciated Property.*

Fair market value is the price at which property would change hands between a willing buyer and a willing seller, neither being under any compulsion to buy or sell, and both having reasonable knowledge of the relevent facts. . . .

REDUCTION FOR CERTAIN INTEREST

Interest prepaid by you, or interest to be paid by you, on a loan secured by property that you donate to a qualified organization must be deducted from the amount of the contribution. The purpose is to avoid a double deduction for interest paid and for a charitable contribution. The amount of the reduction is the amount of the interest that is attributable to the liability assumed by the organization, and that is attributable to any period after the date the contribution was made.

Example. You use the cash method of accounting and you contribute real estate worth $10,000 to the local university.

The bargain sale provision (see *Bargain sales* under *Allocation of Basis*) do not apply in this case. In connection with the contribution, the university agrees to assume your indebtedness of $8,000. You prepaid one year's interest on that indebtedness amounting to $640, and you are planning to take an interest deduction for that amount. The amount of the gift, determined without regard to the rule previously stated, is $2,640 ($10,000 less the $8,000 indebtedness, plus the $640 prepaid interest). The charitable contribution deduction is $2,000, the value of the gift ($2,640) reduced by the $640 allowable as an interest deduction. . . .

GIFTS OF APPRECIATED PROPERTY

If you donate property with a fair market value that is greater than your basis in the property, you may have to reduce the fair market value by all or a portion of the appreciation when computing your deduction. The amount of the reduction depends on whether the property is ordinary income property or capital gain property.

Ordinary income property is property that if it were sold on the date it was contributed would result either in ordinary income or in short-term gain. Examples of ordinary income property are inventory, letters and memorandums given by the person who prepared them (or the person for whom they were prepared), and capital stock held for 9 months or less.

The deduction for a gift of ordinary income is limited to the fair market value less the amount that would be ordinary income.

Example.   You donate to your church stock that you held for 7 months.

The value of the stock is $1,000, but you paid only $800. Since the $200 of appreciation would be short-term gain if you sold the stock, your deduction is limited to $800 (fair market value less the appreciation). . . .

Appraisal fees incurred in determining the fair market value of donated property are not deductible as contributions. However, they may be claimed as miscellaneous deductions on Schedule A (Form 1040). . . .

LIMITATIONS ON DEDUCTIONS

In general, your contributions deduction cannot exceed 50% of your adjusted gross income for the year, line 31 of Form 1040, computed without regard to net operating loss carry-backs. Contributions to most charitable organizations are limited to 50% of your adjusted gross income. However, contributions for the use of any organization, or contributions to certain private non-operating foundations, veterans' organizations, fraternal societies, and nonprofit cemetery companies, are limited to 20% of adjusted gross income. Also, there is a 30% of adjusted gross income limitation that applies to contributions of certain capital gain property. . . .

Public charities include . . . (2) Tax-exempt educational organizations with a regular faculty and curriculum and a regular student body attending resident classes. . . .

For each gift of property for which you claim a deduction of more than $200, you must attach a statement to the return giving the following information:

(1)   The name and address of the donee organization;

(2)   The date of the actual contribution;

(3)   A description of the property in sufficient detail to identify it including, in the case of tangible property, its physical condition at the time of the contribution. In the case of securities, give the name of the issuer, the type of security, and whether it is regularly traded on a stock exchange or in an over-the-counter market;

(4)   The manner and approximate date you acquired the property, for example, by purchase, gift, bequest, etc.;

(5)   The fair market value of the property at the time of the contribution, showing the method used in determining the fair market value. If determined by appraisal, submit a signed copy of the report of the appraiser;

(6)   For appreciated property other than securities, the cost or other basis, as adjusted;

(7)   For certain appreciated property, the amount of the reduction in the value of the contribution and the manner in which the reduction was determined;

(8)   The terms of any agreement or understanding entered into by you, or on your behalf, relating to the use, sale, or other disposition of the property. You must set forth terms of any agreement of understanding that restricts the donee's use of the property or merely earmarks property for a particular charitable use, such as the use of donated furniture in the reading room of the donee's library;

(9)   The amount claimed as a deduction for the tax year as a result of the contribution. If you contribute less than the entire interest in the property during the tax year, give the amount claimed as a deduction in any prior year or years for contribution of other interests in such property, the name and address of each donee organization, the place where the property (if tangible property) is located or kept, and the name of the person having possession of the property if other than the organization to which you contributed the property giving rise to the deduction.

| # List of
Appraisers

The following list of appraisers represents the membership of the Antiquarian Booksellers' Association of America, Inc. It is current to September 1978. All members may be approached for appraisals on a commercial basis, and the association welcomes other inquiries at their headquarters address: 630 Fifth Avenue, Shop 2 Concourse, New York, N.Y. 10020.

The list is arranged geographically by states, alphabetically by city within states, and alphabetically by the first word of entry within cities. Names of individuals within organizations appear directly after the name of the company.

Arizona

Ben Sackheim
5425 East Fort Lowell Road
Tucson, AZ 85712

California

Sand Dollar Books
Jack Shoemaker
1222 Solano Avenue
Albany, CA 94706

J. B. Muns, Books
1162 Shattuck Avenue
Berkeley, CA 94707

Serendipity Books
Peter B. Howard
654 Colusa Avenue
Berkeley, CA 94707

Urban Books
Mrs. James W. McCreary
295 Grizzly Peak Blvd.
Berkeley, CA 94708

Harry A. Levinson
P.O. Box 534
Beverly Hills, CA 90213

The Scriptorum
427 N. Canon Drive
Beverly Hills, CA 90210

Theodore Front
155 North San Vincente Blvd.
Beverly Hills, CA 90211

Donald La Chance
5105 Bridge Street
P.O. Box L
Cambria, CA 93428

Memorabilia, Ltd.
Leon H. Becker
7624 El Camino Real
Carlsbad, CA 92008

Irving Keats
280 Del Mesa Carmel
Carmel, CA 93921

The Talisman Press
Robert Greenwood
P.O. Box 455
Georgetown, CA 95634

Roy V. Boswell
P.O. Box 278
Gilroy, CA 95020

Atlantis Books
H. E. Burroughs
P.O. Box 38202
Hollywood, CA 90038

The Book Treasury
Robert Weinstein
6707 Hollywood Blvd.
Hollywood, CA 90028

Cherokee Book Shop
Jack Blum
6607 Hollywood Blvd.
Hollywood, CA 90028

Larry Edmunds Book Shop
6658 Hollywood Blvd.
Hollywood, CA 90028

Sun Dance Books
1520 N. Crescent Heights
Hollywood, CA 90046

Theodore Reed—Antiquarian Books
P.O. Box 34
Caliente Branch
Julian, CA 92036

Alta California Bookstore
John Swingle
P.O. Box 296
Laguna Beach, CA 92652

Carolyn Kaplan
P.O. Box 201
Laguna Beach, CA 92652

Laurence McGilvery
P.O. Box 852
La Jolla, CA 92037

Art Book Store & Gallery
L. Clarice Davis
1547 Westwood Blvd.
Los Angeles, CA 90024

Barry R. Levin
2253 Westwood Blvd.
Los Angeles, CA 90064

Bennett & Marshall Rare Books
8214 Melrose Avenue
Los Angeles, CA 90046

Caravan Bookstore
605 S. Grand Avenue
Los Angeles, CA 90017

Heritage Book Shop
Ben Weinstein
847 N. La Cienega Blvd.
Los Angeles, CA 90069

Dawson's Book Shop
535 N. Larchmont Blvd.
Los Angeles, CA 90004

Doris Harris—Autographs
5410 Wilshire Blvd.
Los Angeles, CA 90036

George J. Houle
8064 Melrose Avenue
Los Angeles, CA 90046

The Globe Bookstore
Michael R. Geth
P.O. Box 69218
8934 Keith Avenue
Los Angeles, CA 90069

Hollywood Book Shop
Jack Garvin
6613 Hollywood Blvd.
Los Angeles, CA 90028

Galerie Concorde Ltd.
James Normile
6888 Alta Loma Terrace
Los Angeles, CA 90068

Jerrold G. Stanoff, Booksellers
2717 Lakewood Avenue
Los Angeles, CA 90039

June O'Shea
6222 San Vincente Blvd.
Los Angeles, CA 90048

Kurt L. Schwarz
738 South Bristol Avenue
Los Angeles, CA 90049

Kenneth Karmiole, Bookseller
2255 Westwood Blvd.
Los Angeles, CA 90064

Lennie's Book Nook
8125 West 3rd Street
Los Angeles, CA 90048

Needham Book Finders
Stanley Kurman
2317 Westwood Blvd.
Los Angeles, CA 90064

Regent House
Nat Morris
108 N. Roselake Avenue
Los Angeles, CA 90026

Roy Bleiweiss
2277 Westwood Blvd.
Los Angeles, CA 90064

Samuel W. Katz
10845 Lindbrook Drive, Suite 6
Los Angeles, CA 90024

William & Victoria Dailey
Victoria Dailey
P.O. Box 69812
Los Angeles, CA 90069

Zeitlin & Ver Brugge
815 N. La Cienega Blvd.
Los Angeles, CA 90069

Zeitlin Periodicals Co., Inc.
Stanley Zeitlin, Pres.
817 S. La Brea Avenue
Los Angeles, CA 90036

The Joyce Book Shops
Box 310
Martinez, CA 94553

Morningsun Rare Books
Margaret M. Herbring
355 South Morningsun Ave.
Mill Valley, CA 94941

Valley Book City
Jerry Weinstein
5249 Lankershim Blvd.
North Hollywood, CA 91601

The Holmes Book Co.
Craig H. Keyston
274 14th Street
Oakland, CA 94612

Northwest Books
Donald McKinney
3814 Lyon Avenue
Oakland, CA 94601

Palmer D. French
P.O. Box 2704
Oakland, CA 94602

The Book Sail
John McLaughlin
1186 North Tustin
Orange, CA 92667

William Schneider Books
P.O. Box 652
Pacific Grove, CA 93950

International Bookfinders, Inc.
Box 1
Pacific Palisades, CA 90272

William P. Wreden
200 Hamilton Avenue
P.O. Box 56
Palo Alto, CA 94302

Maxwell Hunley
225 S. Los Robles Avenue
Pasadena, CA 91101

Burger & Evans
William J. B. Burger
Gloria Lane—P.O. Box 832
Pine Grove, CA 95665

Argus Books
2741 Riverside Blvd.
Sacramento, CA 95818

Carlos Book Stall
1115 San Carlos Avenue
San Carlos, CA 94070

William Bledsoe, Bookseller
P.O. Box 763
San Carlos, CA 94070

Wahrenbrecks Book House
CA. A. Valverde
649 Broadway
San Diego, CA 92101

Alan Wofsy Fine Arts
150 Green Street
San Francisco, CA 94111

The Albatross & Round-up Book
    Cos.
166 Eddy Street
San Francisco, CA 94102

Antiques Bibliopole
Pauline A. Grosch
4147 24th Street
San Francisco, CA 94114

Argonaut Book Shop
792 Sutter Street
San Francisco, CA 94109

Bernard M. Rosenthal, Inc.
251 Post Street
San Francisco, CA 94108

The Brick Row Book Shop
251 Post Street
San Francisco, CA 94108

Ernest Lubbe—Books
280 Golden Gate Avenue
San Francisco, CA 94102

Jeremy Norman & Co.
442 Post Street
San Francisco, CA 94102

John Scopazzi—Fine & Rare Books
278 Post Street, Suite 305
San Francisco, CA 94108

Louis Collins Books
898 Carolina Street
San Francisco, CA 94107

California Book Auction Galleries
Maurice F. Powers
356 Golden Gate Avenue
San Francisco, CA 94102

Randall & Windle
Ronald R. Randall
185 Post Street
San Francisco, CA 94108

San Francisciana
Marilyn Blaisdell
155 San Anselmo Avenue
San Francisco, CA 94127

John Howell—Books
Warren R. Howell
434 Post Street
San Francisco, CA 94102

Marian L. Gore—Bookseller
Box 433
San Gabriel, CA 91775

Michael S. Hollander
P.O. Box 3678
San Rafael, CA 94902

R. E. Lewis, Inc.
P.O. Box 1108
San Rafael, CA 94902

Drew's Bookshop
Box 163
Santa Barbara, CA 93102

Joseph the Provider Books
903 State Street
Santa Barbara, CA 93101

Milton Hammer Books
819 Anacapa Street
Santa Barbara, CA 93101

Volkoff & von Hohenlohe
Rare Books & Manuscripts
1514 La Coronilla Drive
Santa Barbara, CA 93109

Howard Karno Books
P.O. Box 1813
Santa Monica, CA 90406

L'Estampe Originale
Sandra A. Sofris
P.O. Box 897
Saratoga, CA 95070

B & L Rootenberg—Rare Books
P.O. Box 5049
Sherman Oaks, CA 91403

John W. Caler Publications Corp.
7506 Clybourn Avenue
Sun Valley, CA 91352

J. E. Reynolds
3801 Ridgewood Road
Willits, CA 95490

Natural History Books
Rudolph Wm. Sabbot
5239 Tendilla Avenue
Woodland Hills, CA 91364

Colorado

The Hermitage Book Shop
Robert W. Topp
304 E. Colfax
Denver, CO 80203

Connecticut

John F. Hendsey—Bookseller
5 Woodhaven Drive
Avon, CT 06001

Whitlock Farm—Books
Gilbert Whitlock
Sperry Road
Bethany, CT 06525

Carola Paine Wormser
Alfred W. Paine
Wolfpits Road
Bethel, CT 06801

Douglas M. Jacobs
P.O. Box 363
Bethel, CT 06801

Country Lane Books
Edward T. Myers
Box 47
Collinsville, CT 06022

Angler's & Shooter's Bookshelf
Col. Henry A. Siegel
Route 63
Goshen, CT 06756

William Pinkney III
240 N. Granby Road
Granby, CT 06035

Larry Malis
P.O. Box 211
New Canaan, CT 06840

C. A. Stonehill, Inc.
Robert J. Barry, Jr.
282 York Street
New Haven, CT 06511

East & West Shop, Inc.
Thelma Ziemer
4 Appleblossom Lane
Newtown, CT 06470

Old Mystic Bookshop
Charles B. Vincent
58 Main Street
Old Mystic, CT 06372

Chiswick Book Shop, Inc.
Walnut Tree Hill Road
Sandy Hook, CT 06482

Scarlet Letter Books
P.O. Box 117
Sherman, CT 06784

Charles B. Wood III, Inc.
The Green
South Woodstock, CT 06267

Laurence Witten Rare Books
Box 490
Southport, CT 06490

Books for Collectors
60 Urban Street
Stamford, CT 06905

Rockwell Gardiner
60 Mill Road
Stamford, CT 06903

Paula Sterne—Books
George B. Burgeson
Huckleberry Road RFD #2
West Redding, CT 06896

Cedric L. Robinson
597 Palisado Avenue
Windsor, CT 06095

Delaware

The Windsor Collection
Philip A. Roussel
111 Canterbury Drive
Wilmington, DE 19803

District of Columbia

Booked Up, Inc.
Larry McMurtry
1214 31st St., N.W.
Washington, DC 20007

The Old Print Gallery
James C. Blakely
1212 31st St., N.W.
Washington, DC 20007

Q. M. Dabney & Co.
Michael E. Schnitter
Box 31061
Washington, DC 20031

Oscar Shapiro
3726 Connecticut Ave., N.W.
Washington, DC 20008

Florida

Best Books
Eugene F. Kramer
P.O. Box 731
Hillard, FL 32046

A to Z Book Service
Lucile Coleman
P.O. Box 610813
North Miami, FL 33161

Georgia

Harvey Dan Abrams
739 E. Morningside Drive N.E.
Atlanta, GA 30324

Hawaii

Pacific Book House
Kilohana Square
1016 Kapahulu Avenue
Honolulu, HI 96816

Idaho

The Yesteryear Shoppe
Dave C. Gonzales
1221 1st Street South
Nampa, ID 83651

Illinois

The Old Dragon's Book Den
Janet Mosbacher
P.O. Box 186
Barrington, IL 60010

Canterbury Bookshop
J. F. von Berg
29 East Congress Pkwy.
Chicago, IL 60605

Hamill & Barker
400 N. Michigan Avenue, Room 1210
Chicago, IL 60611

Joseph O'Gara Bookseller
1311 East 57th Street
Chicago, IL 60637

Kenneth Nebenzahl, Inc.
333 N. Michigan Avenue
Chicago, IL 60601

Magic, Inc.
Jay Marshall, Pres.
5082 N. Lincoln Avenue
Chicago, IL 60625

Marshall Field & Co.
Rare Book Dept.
111 N. State Street
Chicago, IL 60690

Owen Davies—Bookseller
Dorothy B. Davies
1214 N. LaSalle Street
Chicago, IL 60610

Kennedy's Bookshop
Ashley Kennedy, III
1911 Central Street
Evanston, IL 60201

Van Norman Book Co.
C. E. Van Norman, Sr.
422-424 Bank of Galesburg Bldg.
Galesbury, IL 61401

The Scholar Gypsy, Ltd.
Thomas J. Joyce
P.O. Box 561
8 South 3rd Street
Geneva, IL 60134

Titles, Inc.
P.O. Box 342
HIghland Park, IL 60035

The Colophon Book Shop
Robert Liska
700 South Sixth Street
La Grange, IL 60525

Van Allen Bradley, Inc.
P.O. Box 578
Lake Zurich, IL 60047

Alec R. Allenson, Inc.
635 E. Ogden Avenue
Naperville, IL 60540

The Book Stall
126 N. Church Street
Rockford, IL 61101

Cogitator Bookstore
Donald Vento
1165 Wilmette Avenue
Wilmette, IL 60091

Leekley Book Search
Evelyn Leekley
P.O. Box 337
Winthrop Harbor, IL 60096

Iowa

McBlain Books
Philip A. McBlain
P.O. Box 971
Des Moines, IA 50304

Kentucky

W. C. Gates, Books
William C. Gates
1279 Bardstown Road
Louisville, KY 40204

Louisiana

Taylor Clark's Inc.
George Taylor Clark, Jr.
2623 Government Street
Baton Rouge, LA 70806

Maine

Lillian Berliawsky—Books
23 Bay View Street
Camden, ME 04843

Patricia Ledlie—Bookseller
Box 46
Buckfield, ME 04220

F. M. O'Brien
34 High Street
Portland, ME 04101

Aimee B. MacEwen—Bookseller
Victorian House
Stockton Springs, ME 04981

Maryland

John Gach Bookshop Inc.
John Gach
3322 Greenmount Avenue
Baltimore, MD 21218

Jeff Dykes—Western Books
Box 38
College Park, MD 20740

Gail Klemm—Books
P.O. Box 551
Ellicott City, MD 24103

Doris Frohnsdorff
P.O. Box 2306
Gaithersburg, MD 20760

Massachusetts

The Printers' Devil
Barry A. Wiedenkeller
One Claremont Court
Arlington, MA 02174

Brattle Book Shop
5 West Street
Boston, MA 02111

Edward Morrill & Son, Inc.
25 Kingston Street
Boston, MA 02111

Goodspeeds Book Shop, Inc.
18 Beacon Street
Boston, MA 02108

Maury A. Bromsen Associates, Inc
770 Boylston Street
Boston, MA 02199

Starr Book Company, Inc.
37 Kingston Street
Boston, MA 02111

The Charles Daly Collection
Barbara Wall
66 Chilton Street
Cambridge, MA 02138

Hoffman & Freeman Antiquarian
   Booksellers
P.O. Box 207
Cambridge, MA 02128

Pangloss Bookshop
1284 Massachusetts Avenue
Cambridge, MA 02138

Templer Bar Bookshop
9 Boylston Street
Cambridge, MA 02138

Edward J. Lefkowicz
P.O. Box 630
Fairhaven, MA 02719

George Robert Minkoff, Inc.
R.F.D. #3, Box 147
Great Barrington, MA 02130

Fonda Books
Box 1800
Nantucket, MA 02554

Christian Verbeke
7 Pond Street
Newburyport, MA 01950

Isaac J. Oelgart
34 Charles Street
Newburyport, MA 01950

The Rendells, Inc.
154 Wells Avenue
Newton, MA 02159

Dwyer's Bookstore, Inc.
Jeffery P. Dwyer
P.O. Box 426, 44 Main Street
Northampton, MA 01060

Michael Ginsberg Books, Inc.
P.O. Box 402
Sharon, MA 02067

Peter L. Stern
P.O. Box 160
Sharon, MA 02067

Howard S. Mott, Inc.
Sheffield, MA 01257

Victor Tamerlis
9 Stanton Avenue
South Hadley, MA 01075

Western Hemisphere, Inc.
Eugene L. Schwaab
1613 Central Street
Stoughton, MA 02072

Paul C. Richards, Autographs
High Acres
Templeton, MA 01468

Harold M. Burstein
16 Park Place
Waltham, MA 02154

Bromer Booksellers
Anne C. Bromer
127 Barnard Avenue
Watertown, MA 02172

William Young & Co.
P.O. Box 282
Wellesley, MA 02181

M & S Rare Books, Inc.
Daniel G. Siegel
Box 311
Weston, MA 02193

Samuel E. Murray
477 Main Street
Wilbraham, MA 01095

Isaiah Thomas Books & Prints
James A. Visbeck
980 Main Street
Worcester, MA 01603

Parnassus Book Service
Route 6a, Box 33
Yarmouth Port, MA 02675

Michigan

The Cellar Book Shop
Mrs. Petra F. Netzorg
18090 Wyoming
Detroit, MI 48221

Donald C. Allen
Box 3
503 N. Elm Street
Three Oaks, MI 49128

Arnold's of Michigan
511 S. Union Street
Traverse City, MI 49684

Minnesota

Leland N. Lien, Bookseller
413 South 4th Street
Minneapolis, MN 55415

Missouri

Glenn Books, Inc.
1227 Baltimore
Kansas City, MO 64105

Dr. William J. Cassidy
109 East 65th Street
Kansas City, MO 64113

Anthony Garnett—Fine Books
P.O. Box 4918
Saint Louis, MO 63108

R. Dunaway, Bookseller
6138 Delmar Blvd.
Saint Louis, MO 63112

New Hampshire

Robert H. Ross, Rare Books
P.O. Box 985
Hanover, NH 03755

Carry Back Books
Donald M. St. John
Dartmouth College Highway
Route 10
Haverhill, NH 03765

Douglas N. Harding
35 East Pearl Street
Nashua, NH 03060

David L. O'Neal Antiquarian
   Bookseller
RRD 1, Box 13
Peterborough, NH 03458

J & J Hanrahan
Edward J. Hanrahan
62 Marcy Street
Portsmouth, NH 03801

Stinson House Books
George N. Kent
Quincy Road
Ruzney, NH 03266

Edward C. Fales
P.O. Box 56
Salisbury, NH 03268

Old Settler Bookshop
Walpole, NH 03608

Richard L. Sykes
P.O. Box 103
Weare, NH 03281

Hurley Books
Route 12
Westmoreland, NH 03467

New Jersey

The Chatham Bookseller
Fred Deodene
38 Maple Street
Chatham, NJ 07928

Harvey W. Brewer
270 Herbert Avenue
Closter, NJ 07624

Heinoldt Books
Theodore H. Heinoldt
Central & Buffalo Avenue
Egg Harbor, NJ 08215

Robert A. Paulson—Bookseller
37 West Street
Englewood, NJ 07631

Rare Book Company
Ralph Geradi
P.O. Box 957
Freehold, NJ 07728

Books-on-File
Mary Snyder
7014 Park Avenue
Guttenberg, NJ 07093

William T. Clermont—Books
87 Rowland Avenue
Hackensack, NJ 07601

Elizabeth Woodburn
Booknoll Farm
Hopewell, NJ 08525

Dr. Milton Kronovet
881 C Balmoral Court
Lakewood, NJ 08701

Patterson Smith
23 Prospect Terrace
Montclair, NJ 07042

Walter J. Johnson, Inc.
355 Chestnut Street
Norwood, NJ 07648

La Scala Autographs
James Camner
P.O. Box 268
Plainsboro, NJ 08536

Joseph Rubinfine
RFD No. 1
Pleasantville, NJ 08232

Witherspoon Art & Book Store
Mary R. Hicks
12 Nassau Street
Princeton, NJ 08540

Ernest S. Hickok
382 Springfield Avenue
Summit, NJ 07901

J. L. Emdin
11 Euclid Avenue
Summit, NJ 07901

Harold R. Nestler, Inc.
13 Pennington Avenue
Waldic, NJ 07463

New Mexico

Nicholas Potter Bookseller
203 E. Palace Ave.
Santa Fe, NM 87501

New York City

Alfred F. Zambelli
156 Fifth Avenue
New York, NY 10010

Applefield Gallery
1372 York Avenue
New York, NY 10021

Argosy Book Stores
116 E. 59th Street
New York, NY 10022

Arthur H. Minters
84 University Place
New York, NY 10003

Barry Scott—Bookseller
15 Gramercy Park South
New York, NY 10003

Benjamin Blom's Cityana
16 East 53rd Street
New York, NY 10022

Black Sun Books
Harney Tucker
667 Madson Avenue, Suite 1005
New York, NY 10021

Brentano's Book Store
586 Fifth Avenue
New York, NY 10036

Broude Brothers, Limited
Dr. Ronald Broude
56 West 45th Street
New York, NY 10036

The Cartographer
114 East 61st Street
New York, NY 10021

Corner Book Shop
102 Fourth Avenue
New York, NY 10003

Dauber & Pine Bookshops, Inc.
66,Fifth Avenue
New York, NY 10011

David Tunick, Inc.
12 East 80th Street
New York, NY 10021

E. Weyhe
794 Lexington Avenue
New York, NY 10021

Ex Libris
Arthur A. Cohen
25 East 69th Street
New York, NY 10021

F. Thomas Heller
308 East 79th Street
New York, NY 10021

Gotham Book Mart & Gallery Inc.
Andreas Brown, President
41 West 47th Street
New York, NY 10036

H. P. Kraus
16 East 46th Street
New York, NY 10017

House of Books, Ltd.
667 Madison Avenue
New York, NY 10021

House of El Dieff, Inc.
139 East 63rd Street
New York, NY 10021

Inman's Book Shop
Nathan Ladden
14 East 60th Street, Room 1002-A
New York, NY 10022

International University
  Booksellers Inc.
Max J. Holmes
30 Irving Place
New York, NY 10003

Irving Zucker—Art Books
256 Fifth Avenue
New York, NY 10001

Isaac Mendoza Book Co.
Walter L. Caron
15 Ann Street
New York, NY 10038

J. N. Bartfield
45 West 57th Street
New York, NY 10019

James Lowe Autographs, Ltd.
667 Madison Avenue, Suite 709
New York, NY 10021

Janet Lehr
45 East 85th Street
New York, NY 10028

John F. Fleming, Inc.
322 East 57th Street
New York, NY 10022

Justin G. Schiller, Ltd.
P.O. Box 1667, FDR Station
New York, NY 10022

K. Gregory
222 East 71st Street
New York, NY 10021

Lathrop C. Harper, Inc.
22 East 40th Street
New York, NY 10016

Lucien Goldschmidt, Inc.
1117 Madison Avenue
New York, NY 10028

M. Dupriest, Inc.
434 Hudson Street
New York, NY 10014

Madeleine B. Stern
P.O. Box 188, Gracie Station
New York, NY 10028

Martin Breslauer, Inc.
P.O. Box 607
New York, NY 10028

Mrs. Mary S. Rosenberg
17 West 60th Street
New York, NY 10023

Old Print Shop, Inc.
Kenneth M. Newman
150 Lexington Avenue
New York, NY 10016

Pageant Book Co.
59 Fourth Avenue
New York, NY 10003

Philip C. Duschnes
699 Madison Avenue
New York, NY 10021

Richard C. Ramer
225 East 70th Street
New York, NY 10021

Robert K. Brown—Art & Books
120 East 86th Street
New York, NY 10028

Rosejeanne Slifer
30 Park Avenue
New York, NY 10016

Samuel Weiser, Inc.
734 Broadway
New York, NY 10003

Scientific Library Service
29 East 10th Street
New York, NY 10003

Seven Gables Bookshop
3 West 46th Street
New York, NY 10036

Sotheby Parke Bernet, Inc.
Anthony Fair
980 Madison Avenue
New York, NY 10021

Stanley Gilman
P.O. Box 131, Cooper Station
New York, NY 10003

Swann Auction Galleries
117 East 24th Street
New York, NY 10010

Trebizond Rare Books
William R. Benedict
667 Madison Avenue
New York, NY 10021

University Place Book Shop
821 Broadway
New York, NY 10003

Ursus Books, Ltd.
Thomas Peter Kraus
667 Madison Avenue
New York, NY 10021

Victoria Book Shop
307 Fifth Avenue, Room 1400
New York, NY 10016

W. S. Heinman
1966 Broadway
New York, NY 10023

William B. Liebmann
211 East 70th Street, Apt. 6B
New York, NY 10021

William H. Schab Gallery, Inc.
37 West 57th Street
New York, NY 10019

William Slater
80 East 11th Street
New York, NY 10003

The Witkin Gallery, Inc.
Lee D. Witkin
41 East 57th Street
New York, NY 10022

Wurlitzer-Bruck
Marianne Wurlitzer
60 Riverside Drive
New York, NY 10024

Ximines Rare Books, Inc.
Stephen Weissman
120 East 85th Street
New York, NY 10028

New York State

Totteridge Book Shop
RD 1—247A North Road
Amenia, NY 12501

J. Howard Woolmer Books
Gladstone Hollow
Andes, NY 13731

E. K. Schreiber—Rare Books
P.O. Box 144
Kingsbridge Station
Bronx, NY 10463

Walter Schatzki
160 Stratford Road
Brooklyn, NY 11218

Sydney R. Smith Sporting Books
Canaan, NY 12029

N & N Pavlov
37 Oakdale Drive
Dobbs Ferry, NY 10522

Bernice Weiss—Rare Books
36 Tuckahoe Avenue
Eastchester, NY 10707

L. W. Currey Rare Books, Inc.
Chuch Street
Elizabethtown, NY 12932

Alexander Hertz & Co., Inc.
88-28 43rd Avenue
Elmhurst, NY 11373

Maxwell Scientific International, Inc.
Dr. Edward Gray
Fairview Park
Elmsford, NY 10523

Roy W. Clare
47 Woodshire South
Getzville, NY 14068

Roger Butterfield, Inc.
White House
Hartwick, NY 13348

Daniel Hirsch—Books
P.O. Box 315
Hopewell Junction, NY 12533

Walter R. Benjamin, Autographs,
    Inc.
Mary A. Benjamin
P.O. Box 255, Scribner Hollow Road
Hunter, NY 12442

Caravan-Maritime Books
87-06 168th Place
Jamaica, NY 11432

Emil Offenbacher
84-50 Austin Street
Kew Gardens, NY 11415

F. A. Bernett, Inc.
2001 Palmer Avenue
Larchmont, NY 10538

Henry Stevens Son & Stiles
1A Albee Court
Larchmont, NY 10538

Howard Frisch
Old Post Road
Livingston, NY 12541

Paul P. Appel
119 Library Lane
Mamaroneck, NY 10543

Kraus-Thomson Organization, Ltd.
Route 100
Millwood, NY 10546

Lubrecht & Cramer
R.F.D. 1
Route 42 & Forestburgh Road
Monticello, NY 12701

Edwin V. Glaser—Rare Books
P.O. Box 1394
New Rochelle, NY 10802

Fordham Book Company
Mrs. Helen Hirsch
Box 6
New Rochelle, NY 10801

William Salloch
Pines Bridge Road
Ossining, NY 10562

Timothy Trace
Red Mill Road
Peekskill, NY 10566

Yankee Peddler Bookshop
John Westerberg
94 Mill Street
Pultneyville, NY 14538

Parnassus Book Shop
Stanley Lewis
Route 9 Old Starr Library
Rhinebeck, NY 12572

The Book Chest
Estelle Chessid
19 Oxford Place
Rockville Center, NY 11570

Paulette Greene—Rare Books
140 Princeton Road
Rockville Center, NY 11570

The Hennesseys
Joseph P. Hennessey
4th & Woodlawn
Saratoga, NY 12866

Lyrical Ballad Bookstore
John DeMarco
7 Phila Street
Saratoga Springs, NY 12866

Nathaniel L. Cowen
2196 Stoll Road
Saugerties, NY 12477

Anne Marie Sahnase
120 Brown Road
Scarsdale, NY 10583

John S. Kebabian
2 Winding Lane
Scarsdale, NY 10583

Hammer Mountain Book Halls
Wayne Somers
771 State Street
Schenectady, NY 12307

Jo Ann Casten
R.R. 2, Little Bay Road
Wading River, NY 11792

Albert J. Phiebig, Inc.
P.O. Box 352
White Plains, NY 10602

The Book Gallery
512 Mamaroneck Avenue
White Plains, NY 10605

A 'Gatherin
Robert Dalton Harris
P.O. Box 175
Wynantskill, NY 12198

Green Thought Booksellers
Robert Frey
283 Lee Avenue
Yonkers, NY 10705

North Carolina

B. L. Means—Books
4200 A Knob Oak Lane
Charlotte, NC 28211

Thomas W. Broadfoot
Rt. 2—Box 28A
Wendell, NC 27591

Ohio

Robert C. Hayman
R.F.D. 1
Carey, OH 43316

Acres of Books, Inc.
633 Main Street
Cincinnati, OH 45202

Paul H. North, Jr.
81 Bullitt Park Place
Columbus, OH 43209

Kendall G. Gaisser
1242 Broadway
Toledo, OH 43609

Oregon

G. A. Bibby—Books
1225 Sardine Creek Road
Gold Hill, OR 97525

Beaver Book Store
Frank Isbell
3747 S. E. Hawthorne Blvd.
Portland, OR 97205

Green Dolphin Bookshop
Wright Lewis
215 S.W. Ankeny Street
Portland, OR 97204

Old Oregon Book Store
Preston McMann
122 S.W. 2nd Avenue
Portland, OR 97204

Pennsylvania

Robert F. Batchelder
1 West Butler Avenue
Ambler, PA 19002

Eric Book Store
717 French Street
Erie, PA 16501

The Family Album
Ronald Lieberman
R.D. 1, P.O. Box 42
Glen Rock, PA 17327

Geoffrey Steele
Bucks County
Lumberville, PA 18933

Ralph T. Howey
Hampton House, 10B
1600 Hagysford Road
Narberth, PA 19072

Charles Sessler, Inc.
1308 Walnut Street
Philadelphia, PA 19107

George S. MacManus Co.
1317 Irving Street
Philadelphia, PA 19107

Schuylkill Book Service
Samuel F. Kleinman
873 Belmont Avenue
Philadelphia, PA 19104

Norman Kane
1525 Shenkel Road
Pottstown, PA 19464

Earl Moore Associates, Inc.
P.O. Box 243
Wynnewood, PA 19096

Rhode Island

The Current Company
Robert Rulen Miller
12 Howe Street
Bristol, RI 02809

South Carolina

Hampton Books
Route 1, Box 76
Newberry, SC 29108

Texas

The Jenkins Company
Box 2085
Austin, TX 78767

Ray S. Walton—Bookseller
P.O. Box 4398
Austin, TX 78745

W. Thomas Taylor—Bookseller
2200 Guadalupe, No. 224
Austin, TX 78705

Walter Reuben, Inc.
410 American Bank Tower
Austin, TX 78701

Fred White, Jr.—Bookseller
P.O. Box 3698
Bryan, TX 77801

Aldredge Book Store
2506 Cedar Springs
Dallas, TX 75201

Conway Barker, Autograph Dealer
4126 Meadowdale Lane
P.O. Box 30625
Dallas, TX 75230

The Wilson Bookshop
Robert A. Wilson
3005 Fairmount Street
Dallas, TX 75201

Vermont

James L. Fraser
309 S. Willard Street
Burlington, VT 05401

John Johnson
R.F.D. 2, Homespun Acres
North Bennington, VT 05257

Richard H. Adelson
Antiquarian Bookseller
North Pomfret, VT 05053

Charles E. Tuttle Co., Inc.
P.O. Drawer F
Rutland, VT 05701

Virginia

Nelson Bond
4724 Easthill Drive
Roanoke, VA 24018

JoAnn Reisler
360 Glyndon Street NE
Vienna, VA 22180

The Bookpress, Ltd.
John R. Curtis, Jr.
P.O. Box K.P.
420 Prince George Street
Williamsburg, VA 23185

Bookworm & Silverfish
James S. Presgraves
P.O. Box 516
Wytheville, VA 24382

Washington

Dave Turner, Books
17008 N.E. 80th Street
Redmond, WA 98052

George H. Tweney—Rare Books
16660 Marine View Drive, S.W.
Seattle, WA 98166

S & N Ottenberg, Booksellers
Simon Ottenberg
P.O. Box 15509, Wedgewood Station
Seattle, WA 98115

The Shorey Book Store
110 Union Street
Seattle, WA 98101

West Virginia

Emily Driscoll
P.O. Box 834
Shepherdstown, WV 25443

Canada

Isobel Mackenzie
900 Sherbrook Street West
Montreal PQ Canada H3A 1G3

Monk Bretton Books
Roderick Brinckman
1 Dale Avenue
Toronto Ont. Canada M4W 1K2

William P. Wolfe
22 Rue de l'Hôpital
Montreal PQ Canada H2Y 1V8

Virgin Islands

Jeltrups' Books
51 ABC Company Street
Christiansted
St. Croix, U.S. Virgin Islands 00820

APPENDIX C | # ACRL Statement of Appraisals

1. The appraisal of a gift to the library for tax purposes generally is the responsibility of the donor who benefits from the tax deduction. Generally, the cost of the appraisal should be borne by the donor.
2. The library should at all times protect the interests of its donors as best it can and should suggest the desirability of appraisals whenever such a suggestion would be in order.
3. To protect both its donors and itself, the library, as an interested party, ordinarily should not appraise gifts made to it. It is recognized, however, that on occasion the library may wish to appraise small gifts, since many of them are not worth the time and expense an outside appraisal requires. Generally, however, the library will limit its assistance to: (a) providing him with information such as auction records and dealers' catalogs; (b) suggestions of appropriate professional appraisers who might be consulted; (c) administrative and processing services which would assist the appraiser in making an accurate evaluation.
4. The acceptance of a gift which has been appraised by a third, and disinterested party, does not in any way imply an endorsement of the appraisal by the library.
5. An archivist, curator, or librarian, if he is conscious that as an expert he may have to prove his competence in court, may properly act as an independent appraiser of library materials. He should not in any way suggest that his appraisal is endorsed by his library (such as by the use of the library's letterhead), nor should he ordinarily act in this fashion (except when handling small gifts) if his institution is to receive the donation.

*Reprinted by permission of the American Library Association from "Statement on Appraisal of Gifts," by the Committee on Manuscripts Collections of the Rare Books and Manuscripts Section, *College & Research Library News* (March 1973). Developed by the Committee on Manuscripts Collections of the Rare Books and Manuscripts Section and approved by the ACRL Board of Directors on February 1, 1973, in Washington, D.C., this statement replaces the 1960 policy on appraisal found in *Antiquarian Bookman*, vol. 26 (December 19, 1960), p. 2205.

Gift Policy
Statements

POLICY ON GIFTS
MARRIOTT LIBRARY
UNIVERSITY OF UTAH*

1. *Rationale.* The Libraries of the University of Utah depend heavily on gifts to enhance the quality of our collections. Donors from all parts of the community and the university have helped immeasurably to enrich the holdings of the library. We will continue to be grateful for the kind of support that has been shown in the past. Gifts may be made both in money and in kind (the latter including books, A-V materials or other items of value). Because of the nature of a research library collection, certain conditions need to be observed when receiving gifts, as noted below.

2. *Gifts of Books.* Ordinarily, the donor will give books, which he/she is willing to remove from their personal library, or which result from the disposal of an estate. The Library will make clear in such a case whether it wishes to accept the books, that it may place books which do not fit into the established collection policy, or books that are duplicates in the collection, on sale; that it may reject certain kinds of gifts (books in unusable condition for example); that it may dispose of certain books by gift to other institutions.

It must also be made clear to the donor that in the ordinary course of events a donated collection of books will not be kept together, but will be distributed throughout the Library in accordance with the Library of Congress classification system.

3. *Gift of Realia.* Ordinarily, the University does not collect or accept as gifts items which are not books or non-print learning materials, since this would tend to make us function as a museum rather than Library. There have been exceptions to this in the past, especially when the items of *realia* have been closely bound up with literary items, for example, a wooden chest containing valuable diaries.

4. *Gifts of Manuscripts and Papers.* The University collects manuscripts and other unpublished materials in certain restricted areas, including but not

*Reprinted by permission of Marriott Library, University of Utah.

limited to early Utah and Mormon diaries, letters pertaining to Western history, etc., and the papers of Utah legislators, Middle East materials and other manuscripts of historical interest.

5. *Gifts of Money.* The Library is prepared to receive gifts of money, and is prepared to allow the donor some latitude in specifying how this money should be spent. The donor may specify certain titles, which will be bought if not already in the Library, and if they fit into the Library's overall acquisitions policy. The donor may also suggest certain areas within the teaching fields of the University, leaving it to the Library to buy books in those areas. We will ordinarily reject money specified for buying books outside the areas of the University's teaching mission, for example in such fields as taxidermy or animal husbandry.

Gifts of money may be made in several ways. The most usual one is to make the gift to the Friends of the Library. Other ways are to give gifts of money in memory of a particular person, living or dead, which may or may not be through the Friends. Gifts of money may also be made to the University Development Office, with a notation that such gifts should be dedicated to Library purchases.

6. *Acknowledgment of Gifts.* All non-trivial gifts either of books or money (a rule of thumb would be anything worth more than $10) will be acknowledged by a letter from the Library, with a copy to the University Development Office. The Development Office will then send an official university form of acknowledgment. In case of gifts exceeding $25 in worth, the donor may be enrolled in the appropriate membership category of the Friends of the Library. There may be cases, such as corporate donations, where such memberships may be deemed inappropriate and be omitted.

7. *Forms of Contributions.* The Library has available a sample form for deeds of gift which transfer title to the books from the donor to the Library. In the case of smaller gifts, a simple letter of intent from the donor will serve the same purpose.

8. *Tax Implications.* The establishment of the gift's value for tax purposes is the responsibility of the donor. The Gifts and Exchanges Librarian, as a representative of the beneficiary, as an interested party, may provide a written opinion giving an appraisal of the value of gifts. However, such appraisal is informal in nature, and may or may not be used for tax purposes.

If the donor wishes a formal appraisal of the gift, the Gifts and Exchange Librarian will supply the names of qualified professional appraisers. Appraisals are made at the donor's expense, but are tax deductible. In special cases, the library may assume the responsibility of finding and paying for an appraiser itself.

Donors who have questions about deductions for gifts should ordinarily be referred to the local office of Internal Revenue Service and to IRS Publication 561/8, which is available in the Documents Collection of the Library.

9. *Solicitation of Gifts.* Solicitation of gifts may be carried on by any interested party within the Library, Friends of the Library, etc. However, ordinary solicitation of gifts will be the primary responsibility of the following:

a. The Gifts and Exchange Librarian will have the majority responsibility of soliciting material from other institutions of higher learning, corporate parties, and federal, state and local government documents, and of coordinating and disseminating information about the efforts described in (b) and (c) below.

b. The Curator of Special Collections materials, who can be expected to play the leading role in solicitation of items connected with major special collections, such as Mormonia, Utahniana, Western Americana, Middle East and the like. Manuscript and other non-print material will ordinarily lie within his/her responsibility.

c. The Friends of the Library will also be responsible for soliciting gifts of money or books.

d. Other Library personnel may be designated by the Administration to solicit gifts.

In solicitation the Library may solicit specific titles or collections, although more general appeals will usually be employed.

In any form of solicitation of gifts it is essential to check with the University's Development Office to assure that we may not be working at cross-purposes with a University gift solicitation. An example of this might be that a donor feels his/her duty toward the University has been done with a $1,000 gift to the Library, when at the same time the University has been dealing with him/her for a much larger donation. Such liaison is the primary responsibility of the librarian initiating the request.

10. *Acknowledgment of Gifts.* Acknowledgment may take several forms, usually dependent on the size of the gift. In all cases there will be a letter of thanks from the Library, with carbon copy to G & E if they are not the originators. Next, books donated may have a pre-printed gift place affixed, with the donor's name filled in. In certain cases, a specific gift plate may be printed with the donor's name or that of the person whom he/she wishes to memorialize by the gift. Further and more elaborate acknowledgment of gifts may be used, such as brochures providing the name of the donor of the gift, and its nature, or naming a collection, room, or entire library after the donor.

11. *Publicizing Gifts.* In the case of gifts of more than ordinary value, the Library may publicize the gift in its quarterly *Newsletter* and the University's public relations office will be contacted to provide further publicity.

12. *Departures from Policy.* Any departures from the policies listed above must receive the approval of the Acquisitions Librarian. If, in his/her judgment, there is a question of policy which cannot be resolved at that level, the matter shall be referred to the Associate Director or Director.

POLICY ON DISPOSAL
MARRIOTT LIBRARY
UNIVERSITY OF UTAH*

BOOK SALE PROCEDURE AND POLICY

Only duplicate materials, library rejects, items not wanted by our exchange partners, gifts of magazines from patrons and library staff are sold at the book sale.

*Reprinted by permission of Marriott Library, University of Utah.

When materials reach the Gifts and Exchanges Division, they are either duplicates, or they are withdrawn from the general collection by subject specialists. All gifts are first inspected by subject specialists and many are added to the general collection. Then, an effort is made by the Gifts and Exchanges staff to exchange many of the duplicate or withdrawn items with other libraries for materials needed by the Marriott Library. Journals are sent to the bindery where many are used to complete sets. It is only after this effort that materials are considered for the book sale.

It is the responsibility of the Gifts and Exchanges division to prepare book sale materials in the following manner:

1. Items are stored on designated shelves in the Gifts and Exchange area.
2. Once a week materials are "de-zapped." This is a simple process—books are whelled on booktrucks to the West Side entrance circulation desk and de-sensitized by the circulation staff.
3. Immediately after the material is de-sensitized and returned to the Gifts and Exchanges area, it is priced. It has been a policy of this division to set prices at a reasonable low level. It is our belief that the primary purpose of the book sale is to dispose of materials not needed by the library and therefore prices should be as attractive as possible to potential buyers.
4. All materials are then stored on bookshelves near the Gifts and Exchanges area until the actual booksale date. An effort is being made to arrange materials into broad subject categories on the shelves.
5. The Supplies Department personnel is responsible for the organization and set-up of the sale. Two days before the sale material is removed from the Gifts and Exchanges area to the auditorium. Here again, an effort is made to arrange all sale items into broad subject categories for the convenience of the library patron.
6. A sneak preview for the library staff one day before the sale has become a tradition. No sales are allowed at this time, however.
7. The book sale lasts two days.

SUBJECT: Gifts and Appraisals

INTRODUCTION:

      The resources of the Columbia University Libraries have been developed in the past through the judicious purchase of materials and the acceptance of many valuable and useful gifts. It is recognized that materials received as gifts are fully as important and valuable as items that are bought, and consequently they are given the same degree of care and expeditious handling as purchases. Gifts both of money and of books, periodicals, and other materials contribute to the development of the Libraries and the support of the University's academic programs. Modest gifts are therefore appreciated in the same way as endowments and gifts of larger amounts.

      The responsibility of the Columbia Libraries to the University's research and instructional functions, the need to maintain bibliographic control over collections, the impact of gift materials on space and processing staff, and all the other elements that contribute to the complex nature of large research libraries, require that certain conditions be observed in accepting gifts. The very complexity of the issues suggests the need for considerable flexibility in addressing gift situations and places particular demands on those involved in the decision process.

POLICY:

      It is the policy of the Libraries that gifts of materials be accepted with the understanding that upon receipt they are owned by the University and become part of the Libraries and that, therefore, the library administration reserves the right to determine their retention, location, cataloging treatment, and other considerations related to their use or disposition.

GUIDELINES:

1. General criteria. Factors to be considered in judging the desirability of accepting a gift of materials include the needs of the collection, convenient availability of the material through interlibrary loan, technical processing costs, location and space, maintenance requirements, accompanying restrictions, and relations with the donor.

2. Solicited gifts. Solicitation of gifts is based on orders received in the Acquisitions Department, recommendations from the library staff and faculty members, publications lists, and alertness to publications that might be available on request. The format of solicitations varies from preprinted forms, typically used for corporate or institutional donors, to personal letters, usually prepared for individual donors.

SUBJECT: Gifts and Appraisals (con't)

   3. Unsolicited gifts. The general criteria for accepting gifts are
       especially applicable to unsolicited gifts. Whether these come
       from organizations or individuals, all are recorded and
       acknowledged.

   4. Appriasals. Donors are encouraged to consider having their gifts
       appraised for income or estate tax purposes. In general, the
       Libraries follow the code on appraisals established by the American
       Booksellers Association. Because the Internal Revenue Service
       may consider a recipient library to be an interested party and
       disallow an evaluation made or paid for by the library, appraisal
       costs are normally borne by the donor. Upon request, the Libraries
       will suggest appropriate persons or organizations to be consulted
       for professional appraisals. The acceptance of a gift which has
       been appraised by a disinterested party does not imply endorsement
       of the appraisal by the Libraries. When the value of the gift is
       nominal and does not warrant the cost of a professional appraisal,
       the Libraries may suggest guidelines or provide such tools as auction
       records and dealer's catalogs which the donor can use in determining
       his own evaluation.

   5. Acknowledgments. Appropriate forms of acknowledgment are made for all
       gifts. These range from signed printed postcards for gifts from
       organizations to signed form letters or personalized letters to
       individuals.

   6. Identifying gifts. All gift materials are identified as such by means
       of an appropriate bookplate before being added to the collection.
       The source is marked on the back of the title page as well, so that
       if the book is rebound in the future the information will be available
       for a new bookplate.

   7. Records of gifts. A card record is made for all gifts and maintained
       by name of donor, indicating the date and description of the gift.
       This record is permanently maintained for gifts from individuals.

   8. Restrictions on gifts. Restrictive conditions as to housing, care,
       access, processing or other limiting factors are usually not
       accepted, in order that gift materials be maximally usable.

   9. Refusing gifts. If it is necessary to decline a gift because it does
       not meet the criteria for acceptance, potential alternative institutions
       or collections are suggested.

SUBJECT: Disposition of Unwanted Materials

INTRODUCTION:

The custodial responsibility of the Libraries imposes a trust to
ensure as distinguished collections for future scholars as we offer the
present academic community. The process of maintaining collections
requires that individual libraries occasionally dispose of materials,
including gifts, which are duplicates, obsolete or otherwise unnecessary
for anticipated research or instructional needs. It is incumbent on
Columbia librarians that decisions regarding the disposal of specific
items be made with the same concern as is exercised in collection building,
so that the integrity of our collections is not impaired, but in fact
may be enhanced.

The Gifts and Exchange Department makes unwanted materials available
to other libraries at Columbia or to other components of the University
that wish to have them. If there is no interest at Columbia, these
materials may be used for exchanges with other institutions, sold to students,
faculty, other institutions or dealers, given to other libraries or in
some other way applied to the University's benefit or good will.

In cases where unwanted materials are sold, the Libraries have an
added responsibility to the University and to donors of maintaining
effective control over the resulting income.

POLICY:

It is the policy of the Libraries to dispose of materials with the
same deliberate attention to University goals as is directed toward the
work of collection development. When unwanted items are sold, the proceeds
shall be returned to the Libraries' Books and Periodicals account unless
responsibility to donors demands that the income be directed to a specific
fund or purpose.

GUIDELINES:

Except for materials believed to be of particular value, or where
a highly specialized market exists for them, final disposition is made
by the Gifts and Exchange Department according to established priorities.
When valuable or highly specialized items are sold directly at auction
or through dealers, proceeds from the sale shall be forwarded to Gifts
and Exchange for deposit unless a specific fund has been established
for a library to receive these credits.

103

Sample
Forms

					Code:	
Date Sent	No.	Date Sent	No.	Date Sent		No.

R47-249-5M

Form 1. A simple exchange record form for materials sent. The code designation in the upper right corner can be either an alpha-numeric code representing the institution or a code representation of the exchange partner's fields of interest. Titles of serials sent regularly are listed on the back.

Date Recd.	No.	Date Ack.	Date Recd.	No.	Date Ack.

R64-249-5M

Form 2. The companion record to Form 1 showing numbers of items received on exchange. Serial titles received regularly are listed on the back.

SERIALS: TITLES RECEIVED		CLAIMS

Institution and Address

Areas of Interest:		
Ed., Phil., Psyc.	Hist., Anthro.	Geog., Poli. Sci.
Relig., Theol.	Bib., L.S., Ref.	Math.
Lit., Ling., Jlm.	Nat. Sci.	Phys., Chem.
F.A., Arch., Mus.	Ap. Sci., Tech.	Bus., Econ.

BOOKS SENT			CORRESPONDENCE SENT	
DATE	NO.	VALUE	DATE	REMARKS
R64(1270)M				

Form 3. Front view of a more sophisticated exchange record form. The card folds in half to a 5-x-8-inch size for filing. The column for "Correspondence Sent" is for recording a very brief record of the history of the exchange activity.

107

BOOKS RECEIVED			CORRESPONDENCE RECEIVED	
DATE	NO.	VALUE	DATE	REFERENCE # AND REMARKS

SERIALS: TITLES SENT	CLAIMS

Form 4. The reverse side of the exchange record which becomes the inside when folded.

GIFTS AND EXCHANGE
COLUMBIA UNIVERSITY LIBRARIES
535 West 114th Street
New York, New York 10027

Gentlemen:

Our exchange records show that we have sent to you and received from you materials on exchange as shown below. It is quite possible that our records are at fault, and we should like to correct them. We should appreciate a reply, indicating your records of our exchange transactions. We also should like to have you fill out the enclosed interest profile, indicating the kinds of materials you would like to receive from us in exchange. Please also indicate your exact mailing address.

May we hear from you soon?

Very truly yours,

Alfred H. Lane, Head
Gifts and Exchange

Materials you have sent us*   *Materials we have sent you**

Serials titles you send us: *Serial titles we send you:*

*Serial issues are not usually included in these figures.

Form 5. This form is used to update exchange records. The space above the salutation is left for the address so that a window envelope may be used, thus eliminating extra typing.

GIFTS AND EXCHANGE
COLUMBIA UNIVERSITY LIBRARIES
535 West 114th Street
New York, New York 10027

Please check below your areas of interest and return with your reply:

Education, Philosophy, Psychology   Natural Sciences

Religion, Theology   Applied Science, Technology

Literature, Linguistics, Journalism   Geography, Political Science

Fine Arts, Architecture, Music   Physics, Chemistry

History, Anthropology   Mathematics

Bibliography, Library Science, Reference Business, Economics

Other: Specify

Form 6. Profile chart to be checked by exchange partner showing subject interests.

EXCHANGE REQUEST	Date
From:	
To:	
Author/editor, title, place, publisher, date	
Remarks (bibliographies checked, etc.)	ISBN
A To be sent back with answer. P.T.O.	

Form 7. International standard exchange request form in triplicate: Part A is to be returned with the reply; part B is to be kept by the recipient; part C is to be kept by the requesting library.

```
EXCHANGE REQUEST                                          Date

From:

To:


Author/editor,  title,  place,  publisher,  date



Remarks (bibliographies checked, etc.)                    ISBN


B        To be kept by the recipient. P.T.O.
```

```
EXCHANGE REQUEST                                          Date

From:

To:


Author/editor,  title,  place,  publisher,  date



Remarks (bibliographies checked, etc.)                    ISBN


C        To be kept by requesting library
```

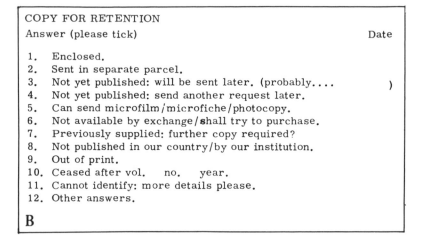

TO BE RETURNED TO REQUESTING LIBRARY

Answer (please tick)   Date

1. Enclosed
2. Sent in separate parcel
3. Not yet published: will be sent later. (probably....   )
4. Not yet published: send another request later.
5. Can send microfilm/microfiche/photocopy.
6. Not available by exchange/shall try to purchase.
7. Previously supplied: further copy required?
8. Not published in our country/by our institution.
9. Out of print.
10. Ceased after vol.   no.   year.
11. Cannot identify: more details please.
12. Other answers.

A

COPY FOR RETENTION

Answer (please tick)   Date

1. Enclosed.
2. Sent in separate parcel.
3. Not yet published: will be sent later. (probably....   )
4. Not yet published: send another request later.
5. Can send microfilm/microfiche/photocopy.
6. Not available by exchange/shall try to purchase.
7. Previously supplied: further copy required?
8. Not published in our country/by our institution.
9. Out of print.
10. Ceased after vol.   no.   year.
11. Cannot identify: more details please.
12. Other answers.

B

Form 8. Reverse side of parts A and B of the request form 7.

DONOR'S NAME									
ADDRESS									

DATE RECEIVED	BOOKS		PAM- PHLETS	UNBD. SERIALS	MISCEL. LANEOUS	ACKNOWLEDGEMENT			EXPLA.
	BD.	UNBD.				DATE	L	1	
									L = Printed Letter; 1 = Post Card

Columbia University Library — GIFT RECORD

Form 9. A gift record card on which the donor's name is entered (last name first, for filing purposes) together with the address to which an acknowledgment will be sent, a count of the number of items received, the date and type of acknowledgment sent.

DATE	IMPORTANT ITEMS
R38 (1275) 5M	

Form 10. The back of the gift record identifies each gift by date and a brief description of the gift (e.g., books in sociology and psychology, OR first editions of American authors, OR the titles if only a few items). A fuller description can be given in the supplementary form shown in Form 11.

113

COLUMBIA UNIVERSITY LIBRARIES

Special Acquisitions Record

Date received _____

This report prepared by_____ Department _____

SOURCE:

Gift of (Name and address of donor) _____

_____ Value _____

Acknowledged (date) _____ BY _____

Exchange from_____ Value _____

Acknowledged (date) _____ BY _____

DESCRIPTION: (to be prepared as soon as possible after receipt by most competent authority on subject available for purpose—donor, member of Library staff, or person recommending acquisition. To be used in report to Trustees, Director's report, publicity, etc.)

For single works give full cataloging entry, subject, significance to scholars, probable use in this library.

For collection state number of manuscripts, books, pamphlets, serials, photocopies, artifacts, etc. Mention items of special importance, subject or subjects covered. Extent of duplication of Library's holdings, significance to scholars, etc.

Form 11. A sample form for giving a more elaborate description of a gift or exchange.

Sehr geehrte Herren!

Wir haben dankend erhalten—We have received with thanks—Nous avons reçu et remercions—Abbiamo rivevuto—Recebenos e agradecemos—Recibimos y agradecemos

---

Es fehlen uns—We are in want of—Il nous manque—Ci mancano—Faltam-nos—Nos faltan

---

Wir senden Ihnen—We are pleased to send you—Nous sommes heureux d'envoyer—Offriamo—Temos o prazer de enviar—Placemos enviarle

---

Wir wurden gern empfangen—We would like to receive—Nous serions heureux de recevoir—Gradiremmo avere—Obsequio enviarnos—Deseamos recibir

---

Wir bitten un austausch—Exchange is requested—On prie de bien vouloir etablir l'echange—Si chiede in cambio—Solicitamos permuta—Deseamos establecer canja

---

Hochachtungsvoll

Form 12. A multilingual, multipurpose form.

COLUMBIA UNIVERSITY LIBRARIES

Gifts and Exchange   Telephone: 280-3532
535 West 114th Street
New York, N.Y. 10027

   The items you recently selected from our disposable materials have been examined and priced at \$_____. If you agree to this price, please make payment to the order of Columbia University and send to the address above.

( ) Materials will be shipped to you, and packing and shipping charges of \$_____ should be added to your payment.

( ) Please arrange to have these materials removed at your earliest convenience.

Next sale period begins_____.

Previous charges unpaid \$_____

Present charges   \$_____

Total due   \$_____

Stat:_____   Date:_____

Form 13. A sample invoice form to be used for sales of books to dealers. "Stat" in the lower left corner is for recording the number of items sold for statistics and is intended only for internal use and does not appear on the copy sent to the buyer.

GIFTS AND EXCHANGE
COLUMBIA UNIVERSITY LIBRARIES
535 West 114th Street
New York, New York 10027

_____   Date _____

_____   Invoice No. _____

_____

_____

Make all checks payable to COLUMBIA UNIVERSITY and mail to the address shown above. Receipt will not be sent unless requested.

_____

_____

Your Order No. or Ref.:_____   Credit: _____

Form 14. General invoice form which can be used to replace Form 13 or to bill for any product or service.

Index

About the Author

Alfred H. Lane is Head of Gifts and Exchanges for the libraries of Columbia University in New York City. He has contributed numerous articles to professional journals.